One South

One South

An Ethnic Approach to Regional Culture

John Shelton Reed

Louisiana State University Press
Baton Rouge and London

Designer: Joanna Hill
Typeface: Bookman
Typesetter: Graphic Composition

Library of Congress Cataloging in Publication Data

Reed, John Shelton.
  One South.

  Bibliography:p.
  Includes index.
  1. Southern States—Civilization. 2. Southern States
—Social conditions. 3. Southern States—Ethnic
relations. 4. Minorities—Southern States. I. Title.
F216.2.R43   975   81-19387
ISBN 0-8071-1003-5 (cloth)   AACR2
ISBN 0-8071-1038-8 (paper)

Third printing (January, 1994)

This one's for Sarah,
Tarheel born and bred;
and for Dale, as always.

Contents

Figures and Tables

Preface and Acknowledgments

While putting together a National Endowment for the Humanities Summer Seminar in 1980, it occurred to me that a number of articles and essays that I had written during the 1970s hung together pretty well as examples of what I flattered myself by thinking was a coherent and sensible approach to the study of the modern South. LSU Press has won my eternal gratitude by agreeing (but then they are, as I have discovered, thoroughly agreeable people).

Twelve of the thirteen chapters in this collection have been published before in some form or other, although in such a variety of places (and some of them so obscure) that I would be mightily impressed if anyone had already encountered even most of them. Although I think these essays are linked to one another by their content, the style is unfortunately another matter. They were written originally for a variety of audiences and situations: speeches to community groups, seminar papers, articles in professional journals of sociology. In consequence, they range in style from the sprightly (some might say frivolous) to the sober (not to say ponderous). My only gesture toward harmonizing them has been to remove repetition where possible and (on the advice of Beverly Jarrett) to cut down drastically on the scholarly apparatus of citation and footnote, where it was present to begin with. In general, I have tried to include enough information in the text so that the assiduous reader can use the bibliography to track down references, comforting myself by reflecting that fuller documentation is usually available in the original publication, for those who care.

Many people must share whatever credit or blame attaches to this collection. Most obviously, I am indebted to my colleague and friend, Merle Black, the instigator and senior author of "Blacks and Southerners" and author of the article to which "Summertime and the Livin' Is

Easy" is something of a rejoinder. Glen Elder barely escaped being coauthor of "Getting To Know You," and we worked together on the Survey of North Carolina, analyzed in that article and alluded to elsewhere. In my twelve years at Chapel Hill, I've had the pleasure of working with some outstanding undergraduates, and material from their term papers and senior honors essays has made its way into four of these articles. I thank Cameron Ingram for his contribution to "The Heart of Dixie"; Janice Coulter for her work cited in "Max Weber's Relatives and Other Distractions"; Gail Wood for her study, the basis for "Getting To Know You"; and Raymond Manley Strunk for some material incorporated into "Below the Smith and Wesson Line."

Several of these chapters were written more or less to order for the symposiums on the South that are such a delightful feature of our cultural landscape. I thank the organizers of these muse-ins for their hospitality, and for forcing me to sit down and organize my thoughts on some subject. Several of the more recent articles were written during a year in which I had a Guggenheim Fellowship to work on something else altogether. I take this opportunity to thank the Guggenheim Foundation for its inadvertent support, and to assure it that the other project will be completed in the fullness of time. This book would have been impossible without the technical services of the Institute for Research in Social Science, the superb clerical assistance of my department's secretarial staff (especially that of Anna Tyndall and Priscilla MacFarland), the financial support of the National Science Foundation for the Survey of North Carolina, and the editorial help of DeAnn Judge in Chapel Hill and of the staff of the LSU Press in Baton Rouge. I want especially to thank Catherine Barton, whose copy-editing skill is equaled only by her tact in dealing with an author who tends to get cranky when corrected.

It is impossible to list those to whom I have intellectual debts. I hope, in some cases, that the debt is obvious. Students of the South are a remarkably congenial and helpful group, and I have spent many pleasant hours talking with historians, political scientists, anthropologists, literary critics, geographers, "religionists," and journalists, as well as sociologists—in Chapel Hill, throughout the South, across the United States, and even overseas. I am afraid to begin a list that would either go on for pages or leave someone out, but I would like to record a special debt to the participants in that NEH Summer Seminar, who not only got me thinking about putting this book together and provided valuable criticism but were a delightful group of people.

I must, finally, thank my colleagues in the sociology department of the University of North Carolina, Chapel Hill, for their tolerance— indeed, encouragement—of what must strike some of them as a strange brand of sociology. I'm pleased that they recognize and value the department's past contributions to the South's understanding of it- self, and tremendously gratified that they think my work is in that fine tradition.

For permission to reprint the essays, I am grateful to the original publishers, as follows: "Whatever Became of Regional Sociology?" published originally as "Sociology and Regional Studies in the United States," *Ethnic and Racial Studies*, III (January, 1980), 40–51. Re- printed by permission of the publishers, Routledge & Kegan Paul Ltd. "Max Weber's Relatives and Other Distractions: Southerners and So- ciology," from John Shelton Reed and Merle Black (eds.), *Perspectives on the American South* (New York: Gordon and Breach Science Pub- lishers, 1982), II. "The Heart of Dixie: An Essay in Folk Geography," from *Social Forces*, LIV (June, 1976), 925–39, and "Getting To Know You: Regional Stereotyping Among Southern Whites," published origi- nally as "Getting To Know You: The 'Contact Hypothesis' Applied to the Sectional Beliefs and Attitudes of White Southerners," *Social Forces*, LIX (September, 1980), 123–35, both reprinted by permission of *Social Forces* and the University of North Carolina Press. "The Car- dinal Test of a Southerner?" published originally as "'The Cardinal Test of a Southerner': Not Race but Geography," *Public Opinion Quar- terly*, XXXVII (Summer, 1973), 232–40. "Shalom, Y'All: Jewish Southerners," published originally as "Ethnicity in the South: Some Observations on the Acculturation of Southern Jews," *Ethnicity*, VI (1979), 97–106. "Blacks and Southerners," published originally as Merle Black and John Shelton Reed, "Blacks and Southerners: A Re- search Note," *Journal of Politics*, XLIV (February, 1982). Reprinted also by permission of Merle Black. "Grits and Gravy: The South's New Middle Class," originally published as "Grits and Gravy: Observations on the South's New Business and Professional People," in *Southern Business: The Decades Ahead* (Indianapolis: Bobbs-Merrill, 1981). "Plastic-Wrapped Crackers: Southern Culture and Social Change," originally published as "Instant Grits and Plastic-Wrapped Crackers:

Southern Culture and Social Change," in Louis D. Rubin, Jr. (ed.), *The American South: Portrait of a Culture* (Baton Rouge: Louisiana State University Press, 1979). "Below the Smith and Wesson Line: Southern Violence," originally published as "Below the Smith and Wesson Line: Reflections on Southern Violence," in Merle Black and John Shelton Reed (eds.), *Perspectives on the American South* (New York: Gordon and Breach Science Publishers, 1981), I. "Summertime and the Livin' Is Easy: Quality of Life in the South," from *University of North Carolina News Letter*, LIX (December, 1974), 1–4. "The Same Old Stand?" reprinted from Fifteen Southerners, *Why the South Will Survive*, © 1981 by the University of Georgia Press.

Excerpt from the song "Kate," by Marty Robbins, used by permission of the publisher, Mariposa Music, Inc.

One South

Introduction

*If it can be said that there are many Souths, the fact
remains that there is also one South.*

W. J. Cash

Metternich, it is said, once dismissed Italy as "a geographical
expression." Events—and Italians—proved him wrong. Churchill, who
should have known better, said the same thing about India. Wrong
again. For at least a century now, people have been saying something
similar about the American South. The "New South" journalist Henry
Watterson even used the same formula: the South is "simply a geographic expression." The best that can be said about these folks is that
they've been in good, if mistaken, company. The only thing at all unusual about them is that so many have been natives of the territory in
question.

The work I have been doing since the publication in 1971 of a book
called *The Enduring South* is based on the conviction that the South
remains as much a sociological phenomenon as a geographical one.
Despite the determination of most publishers to spell *Southern* with a
lowercase *s*, I believe that the South is still a cultural and cognitive
reality of considerable, and in some ways increasing, importance.

The essays contained in this collection deal with "one South"—in
two senses. In the first place, they are about one South in that they are
about *my* South, a region that is the home of a "quasi-ethnic" regional
group. (I'd have used the title "The Ethnic Southerners," but it was
already taken.) Others have examined their Souths: a congeries of diverse ethnic communities, a set of social classes and racial castes, a
"semiperipheral" economic actor in the capitalist world-system, a geographical entity of bewildering complexity, a collection of unfavorable
statistics, the eastern end of the Sun Belt, the northern tip of a Central
American/Caribbean plantation region, a vintage crying out for tram-
pling. There are a great many ways to look at the South, most of them
useful for some purpose or another. But, whether wisely or not, I
picked my approach in *The Enduring South*, and I have spent the

decade since that book was published exploring some of its implications. The first essay in this volume outlines that approach and, in its terms, summarizes some of what we know and indicates what we don't.

The second sense in which these essays treat one South is that of W. J. Cash, as expressed in my epigraph, taken from *The Mind of the South*. That book was published in 1941, and even then, Cash observed, there were people, "usually journalists or professors," who claimed that the South was only "a figment of the imagination"—that the region was so varied internally and so little different, as a whole, from the rest of the country that it was merely, in other words, a geographical expression. Cash added that "nobody, however, has ever taken them seriously. And rightly."

There are still journalists and professors who say that sort of thing, and it may be that they get a more respectful hearing now. Sometimes they have a point. Reading about the South, I'm often reminded of a *New Yorker* cartoon from a few years back, which showed a group of blind men—one clutching a rope, another embracing a tree trunk, a third with his hand against a garden wall, and so forth. Each was saying, "It's an elephant!" How often someone writes or speaks about the Alabama Black Belt, the Carolina Piedmont, eastern Kentucky, Atlanta, or Nashville, and exclaims, in effect, "It's the South!" Others with a more extensive view have rightly criticized this approach. But if they question whether the elephant is actually there—well, then Cash and I part company with them.

Certainly, if you look at the whole South long enough, it goes all indistinct around the edges. If you continue to stare, even the middle can seem to melt and flow away. But this is true of any social phenomenon. We're told that Samuel Johnson, when asked about Bishop Berkeley's hypothesis that physical reality is an illusion, replied, "I refute him—thus!"—and kicked a stone. We can't do the same when someone questions the existence of *social* facts, but we can be sure that they will be stumbling blocks sooner or later—they'll trip us up somehow—if we ignore them. Ask Metternich. Ask Churchill.

To grant that there are many different parts of the South, many aspects to it, many ways to view it, many conclusions—even contradictory ones—to be drawn from observing it; to grant that it is complex and variegated and that our ideas of and about it will necessarily be oversimplifications, at best; to grant, with David Potter, that it is something of "a sphinx on the American land," always answering our questions, but seldom unequivocally—to grant all this is not to deny that it exists, but rather presupposes that there is something there to talk about. Some of these essays attempt to demonstrate as much, while others simply assume it.

There is little attention here to variation within the South or to conflict among its constituent groups; to the ways it is becoming more like the rest of the country, or its parts are becoming less like each other; to the "many Souths" that unquestionably exist. It is not that I think they're unimportant, but that the other side of the coin—the South as a whole, in the context of the United States—seems more likely these days to be ignored, and, in any case, strikes me as more interesting. To the extent that the South remains cohesive and distinctive, to the extent that we can still speak of one South, we are witnessing in some sense the triumph of history over the centrifugal forces of geography and economics.

The same is true of any ethnic or quasi-ethnic group, of course. The first chapter of this book, "The Sociology of Regional Groups," explores what it means to think of regional groups in these terms—that is, as similar in important ways to those immigrant communities that Americans more often think of as ethnic groups. Although nearly all of the examples come from the study of the American South, the approach should be applicable to the study of any regional (or for that matter national) group, insofar as it is, in fact, a *group*.

The second chapter also looks at sociologists looking at the South. It was written after I discovered (I'm embarrassed to say how late) the flourishing school of regional studies associated with Howard Odum and his colleagues in the 1930s and 1940s, and began to wonder why nobody had ever mentioned them when I was in graduate school in the 1960s. "Whatever Became of Regional Sociology?" argues, implicitly at least, that there are lessons for regional studies in the history of that earlier movement. When it was published, I tacked on a conclusion attempting to account for what I see, perhaps wishfully, as renewed interest in regional topics among American sociologists. (It may be of interest that the essay was published in a British journal devoted largely to studies of ethnic and regional nationalism.)

"Max Weber's Relatives and Other Distractions" looks at the relation between sociology and the South the other way around, examining not what sociologists think about the South, but vice versa. It asks why there have been so few good sociologists from the South and is included here, not because that question is of compelling interest, but because the answer it proposes—that sociology seems to be a Yankee way of knowing—suggests some interesting things about Southern culture.

Part II, "Exploring Southern Identity," turns from disciplinary navel gazing to examine a topic at the heart of the ethnic approach to regional studies, the question of group identity, without which there is no regional group to study. Each of the three chapters in this section looks at some aspect of what Howard Odum's teacher, Franklin Giddings, called "consciousness of kind," and each demonstrates, I hope, how the study of regional groups can contribute to broader theoretical concerns in the social sciences. "The Heart of Dixie" argues that, for sociological purposes, the geographers have it backwards; the South should be defined by locating Southerners, not the other way around. Since this article was published, Wilbur Zelinsky has used its technique to map a number of other American regions, with extremely interesting results.

"The Cardinal Test of a Southerner?" looks at one of the ideological correlates of regional identification, asking whether *Southernness* is a code word for racism, as some have suggested. I find its conclusion cheering. Another correlate of group identification is the belief that one's group is different. "Getting To Know You" looks at how exposure to non-Southerners shapes Southerners' perceptions of regional differences, and replicates the findings of an earlier study that had some surprising results.

On the edges of any group are people who are interesting out of all proportion to their numbers. The issues raised by an ethnic approach to the South are thrown into sharp relief when we look at those who may or may not be Southerners—or, rather, who are Southerners for some purposes but maybe not for others. The chapters in Part III, "Southernness at the Margins," look at three of these borderline cases and ask the questions of identification and cultural coloration that immediately occur to the student of regional groups.

"Shalom, Y'All" examines Southern Jews, or Jewish Southerners (it turns out that either phrase is accurate). If being both Southern and Jewish is sometimes a difficult balancing act, it seems that in other ways one identity reinforces the other. "Blacks and Southerners" (written with Merle Black) examines trends in regional identification among black Southerners. Now more than ever, it appears, there is one South. But does it make sense to use the word *Southerner* for someone living in a setting that might as well be California? "Grits and Gravy" discusses the fact that our folklore simply cannot deal with the large and growing Southern middle class, and asks in what ways middle-class Southerners are still Southern.

The essays in the final part, "The South Today," are linked less by their content than by the fact that they are more explicitly exhortative than the previous chapters. From time to time, I get the opportunity to write about what I like and dislike about the South, and it is hard to resist. Unlike some of the earlier essays, none in this section pretends to scholarly objectivity. "Plastic-Wrapped Crackers," contributed to a Voice of America symposium, summarized for an indistinct but presumably foreign audience both the reasons for supposing that Southern cultural distinctiveness is decreasing and the evidence that, in some respects, it isn't. It ends with what my old rhetoric teacher would have called a "pious hope conclusion," giving some not very persuasive reasons for hoping that the South will survive urbanization and industrialization in better shape than the Northeast. "Below the Smith and Wesson Line" is an attempt to go beyond simply deploring Southern violence, to understand it as an exaggerated form of a cultural trait that I, at least, rather admire. Obviously (I hope), to admire the trait is not to admire its excesses. Lynchings and bombings are the kind of thing that give Southern violence a bad name.

When Merle Black discovered that Southerners believe the South to be a superior place to live, his Texas populist soul was scandalized. I thought, and still do, that Southerners are right, and "Summertime and the Livin' Is Easy" is an installment in my continuing argument with Merle. Finally, "The Same Old *Stand*?" was written for a symposium marking the fiftieth anniversary of *I'll Take My Stand*, and was intended to be in the spirit of that Agrarian manifesto (although it may strike some readers as sounding like a less tormented and less talented version of W. J. Cash). Its first half describes, anecdotally, the sorts of experiences that can produce both regional chauvinism and an interest in the ethnic approach to regional studies. In the second half, I throw caution to the wind for a string of speculations about what is happening to Southern culture.

I hope that this collection as a whole, and some of the essays in particular, will be taken as contributions to sociology, if not to resuscitate the moribund field of regional sociology, at least to remind my colleagues of a basis for group formation that we have been inclined to neglect of late. But I recognize that most of these chapters are less works of sociology than sociologically informed musings about the region that is my home. I imagine that most readers will not be sociologists, and that many will be Southerners. Southerners, I note in Chapter 3, tend to be skeptical about sociology, but I urge any skeptics who pick up this volume to suspend their prejudices long enough to examine and weigh this sociological approach to studying their—our—region. I obviously believe it can produce interesting results, and I hope they come to agree.

I.   Sociology in and of the South

1.   The Sociology of Regional Groups

Groups identified by their association with regions of the United States—Southerners, New Englanders, and the like—are similar in some respects to groups more usually thought of as ethnic, but their membership can cut across conventional ethnic lines. These facts raise some interesting questions for the student of American group life. How does a population inhabiting some terrain become a regional *group*? How do such groups come to see themselves, and to be seen by others, as "different"? How, in fact, are they different, and how did they get that way? How does regional identification interact and compete with other loyalties—national, subregional, or ethnic, for example? What is the effect of migration, and what becomes of the children of migrants? What institutions shape and transmit regional culture and identity? It is not difficult, either methodologically or politically, to study American regional groups; but, despite that, we know surprisingly little about them. In fact, with an exception or two, it is hard even to say what the important groups, in this sense, *are*.

Neither identifying the major American regions nor the correlation of groups to the regions, once identified, is straightforward. The word *region* has many different meanings, and the United States has been subdivided according to historical settlement patterns, networks of communications and commerce, the distribution of natural resources and the economic activities dependent on those resources, cultural characteristics, social and economic problems, administrative convenience, and many other criteria. The result has been a bewildering variety of schemes, of which only a few are worth mentioning here.

For obvious reasons, the regional division used by the Bureau of the Census is one of the most frequently encountered. For gross comparisons, the bureau uses four regions, probably the minimum concession to American diversity, recognizing the Northeastern, Southern, Central, and Western states. For more refined applications, these four regions are subdivided to yield nine (three subregions for the South and two each for the other regions). The bureau's definitions appear to be based on a combination of common sense and historical precedent, with the latter dominating in the case of Delaware, Maryland, and the District of Columbia, which are included in the South.

Most other "regionalizations" have yielded a number of regions somewhere between the bureau's four and nine. For instance, Howard Odum's *Southern Regions of the United States*, attempting to identify areas with common sets of social problems, distinguished six regions; Wilbur Zelinsky's *Cultural Geography of the United States* identified five major regions, on the basis of historical settlement patterns; and in Joel Garreau's *Nine Nations of North America*, eight impinge on the United States. (Garreau solved the always troublesome problem of southern Florida by putting it with the Bahamas and the Caribbean.) In *Cultural Regions of the United States*, however, Raymond Gastil came up with eleven regions in the contiguous United States (Pennsylvania and metropolitan New York are both regions in their own right), probably the largest number one can keep in mind before succumbing altogether to geographical particularism.

There is somewhat more overlap among these results than this summary may suggest. The problem of border areas unavoidably leads to differences, but by and large where there is disagreement, it is because one regional division treats as separate regions what another regards as subregions within a larger region. Zelinsky's West, for example, includes three of Odum's regions, while Odum's Northeast includes two of Zelinsky's. The one common feature of most of these efforts is an approximately agreed-upon South; although Odum excludes Oklahoma and Texas, only the Census Bureau includes anything north of Virginia.

For the student of regional groups, however, these geographical exercises have conceptual problems more serious than the technical ones. He is not interested in regions per se, and the relation of regions defined in these terms to the existence of regional groups is, at best, that of cause and effect, and is sometimes not ascertainable at all. Although the sorts of things usually employed to identify regions can affect the emergence and maintenance of regional groups, inferring the existence of one from the other is, to put it no more strongly, rather indirect.

A more promising approach to identifying significant regional groups is through the study of political sectionalism, as in the work of Ira Sharkansky (see, for instance, *Regionalism in American Politics*). When regional groups come in conflict, the Constitution of the United States almost guarantees that their differences will be expressed politically. However, although historians and political scientists have indeed paid a great deal of attention to sectionalism, they have not usually had this problem in mind. Clearly, the definition of politically important American sections has changed over time, from the trichotomy of New England, Middle States, and South of the early federal period, to the North, South, and West of the middle and late nineteenth century, to the division between the Sun Belt and the rest of the country, which some claim to see emerging today. Just as clearly, the South, in one form or another, has been a fairly fixed star in the sectional constellation. But beyond that it is difficult to say much.

And even this tack must seem unnecessarily oblique to someone interested in a region primarily as the home of a regional group. From that point of view, the question is, in the first place, less geographical than social-psychological; it is less that Southerners are people who come from the South, for instance, than that the South is where Southerners come from. The criteria for membership in a regional group have more to do with identification than with location. The obvious first task is to specify the salient regional groups. Then, perhaps, their habitats can be mapped.

The sort of "folk geography" that moves from the regional group to the region, not vice versa, is beginning to receive some attention, but only for the South do we have anything approaching a regional definition in these terms (although other sorts of groups with strong regional ties, like the Mormons, have been studied this way). As it happens, the "folk" South greatly resembles the Southern region defined by quite different criteria, but even for the South there are discrepancies around the border. As for other regional groups, we have very little basis now for saying even what they are, much less where they are. It seems unlikely, however, that their regional homes will be as clearly delineated as the South.

Studying regional groups as *groups* avoids some difficulties, but not all, by any means. The question of subregions, for example, which plagues other approaches, is still a problem. Within any supposed regional group, there may well be subregional groups with a more vigorous group life, subculture, and claim on their members' loyalties than the more inclusive group. These subregional groups may even define themselves, in part, in opposition to the larger group. (The phenomenon of Southern mountain Republicanism suggests as much about Appalachian whites in relation to white Southerners generally.) But this merely emphasizes the point that the choice of an appropriate "level" of regional division should be made empirically, on grounds of identification, culture, and group life, not based on prior judgments about what groups are important. The general problem, of which this is a special case, does not usually forestall inquiry in other contexts: Does—or rather when does—one speak of Sicilians, for example, rather than Italians, or Jamaicans rather than West Indians?

A related question, perhaps more troublesome, is the extent to which the regional group includes members of minority racial, religious, or ethnic groups within the region. Are Southern blacks, for instance, "Southerners," in any important sense? If there is a regional group based on New England, are the Irish, Italians, and Québecois of that region now to be considered "Yankees"? Again, the answers must be based on the answers to other questions: Do members of the minority groups consider themselves to be also members of the regional group? How many do, in what circumstances? To what extent is this identification accepted by the rest of the regional group?

Regional group membership does not logically preclude membership in such minorities, but obviously some combinations are harder to maintain than others. If the unusual combinations make classification more difficult, they also provide opportunities for insight into the nature of group identity. If, as some have argued, the assimilation of European immigrants has been more thoroughgoing in the South, is this simply because there have been fewer of them? Or is there some other reason why it is easier to remain "New York Irish" than "Irish-Southern"?

The study of regional subcultures raises similar problems. "The culture of New England" usually means that of the region's white Protes-

tants, and the same is true of the phrase "Southern culture." "The culture of the American West" does not, as a rule, mean that of the
region's Oriental, Hispanic, or Native American peoples, although their
influence on the culture of the majority is sometimes recognized.
Whether members of minority groups identify with a regional group as
well, however, the possibility of regional effects on their own subcultures must be allowed, and should be investigated. We know very little
about how regional influences interact with ethnic influences to shape
the culture of a minority group within a region, although it is clear that
they do. Attitude surveys of black Americans during the 1960s, for
example, revealed (almost inadvertently) striking differences between
Southern and non-Southern blacks. My own study of American Jews
has found some regional differences of the same sort and magnitude as
those among white Protestants; the effects of region and religion, that
is, simply add up. But we cannot assume that this will always be the
case; sometimes, presumably, one factor will "wash out" the other. But
a great deal more descriptive research is needed before we can even
say when that happens, much less *why*.

It is no accident that most of what we know about regional identification and regional effects on culture comes from studies of Southerners (indeed, from studies of *white* Southerners—a limitation that
should be kept in mind below). Southerners are, arguably, the most
self-conscious and distinctive of the major American regional groups
and have therefore received more attention than the others, at least
explicitly. (Certainly we know a great deal about the Northeast, but
studies of that region are seldom seen as "regional"; they are, rather,
thought to be "American.")

Obviously, an essential first task is to find out what other regional
groups actually exist, as groups. And we should not let the word *regional* prejudice the outcome; it could be that Texans, Californians,
and metropolitan New Yorkers, to take three likely examples, are seen
and see themselves as sufficiently distinct from other Americans to
qualify. Once such groups are identified, the way will be open for the
comparative study of the topics suggested here, and it seems likely
that the phenomena and processes found among Southerners will be
found, at least in attenuated form, within other regional groups. Already, some theoretical considerations are clear, some obvious ques-

tions can be raised, and a few answers are available—enough to suggest that the questions are important.

Identification with a Regional Group

In the first place, what, exactly, distinguishes a regional group from a mere geographical category? The answer, implicit above, is that a regional group ordinarily enlists the *identification* of its members. It serves them as a reference group, to which they feel they belong, and is not just a classification that happens to include them. This is clearly a matter of degree; some categories are more "grouplike" than others, in that more of their members identify with them more strongly. A little can be said about how such identification comes about.

For a geographical category to serve as the base for a regional group (indeed, for any category to give rise to a group), its label must be meaningful to most people, and they must be able to say with some reliability who belongs and who does not. Some functional and administrative "regions" could not give rise to regional groups; too few know where they are. (Who knows, for instance, which judicial circuit, Federal Reserve District, or amateur radio call-sign area he is in?) Even in the case of better-known categories, some individuals lack the cognitive equipment to locate themselves in what would seem to be the obvious slot. There are residents of the South, for instance, for whom the word *Southerner* has, literally, no meaning; in consequence, it can probably not be taken to apply to them. Certainly, they cannot be said to identify with the regional group. (Such persons are most often old, rural, poorly educated, or some combination of these, and for them the alternative to regional identification is not nationalism, but even greater localism.) At the other extreme would be the person, presumably hypothetical, who is constantly aware of the existence of the category and is able to say with some precision what its boundaries are. Some Southerners, for example, say they give a great deal of thought to their group; further inquiry shows that they are likely to have had their "consciousness raised" by education, media exposure, and, particularly, exposure to non-Southerners.

But knowing that a category exists and that one is in it is not sufficient to produce identification. Residents of the Eastern time zone, for example, probably know who they are, but cannot be said to be a regional group. A resident of California can regard himself and be regarded by others as a Southerner or a Midwesterner or a New Englander, but not as someone identified with the Eastern time zone. (Indeed, the absence of a noun for that concept indicates its vacuity.) One's residential history, and one's family's, play a major role in producing and validating regional identity, a role analogous to that of ancestry in ethnic identity. But these biographical data are not completely determining. Individual perceptions also affect the object and the strength of identification, in particular, perceptions of *similarity* to other members of the regional group and perceptions of *interdependence* with them.

Members of a group may believe that they share certain characteristics that set them off from others, and this belief, whether accurate or not, can serve as a basis for identification. The relation of this perception to the facts of group difference may be very tenuous, particularly in periods of rapid social or cultural change, but we must allow the possibility that perceptions of group differences are to some degree accurate. If they are, at least two implications follow. First, interaction within the group may indeed be more comfortable than interaction across group boundaries. In the words of a question sometimes used to measure group identification, members of a group may well "feel closer to [other group members] than to other people," other things equal. Second, interaction with those who are not members of the group may produce stereotypes about group differences where none existed before. Thus, there is some evidence that the more experience Southerners have had with non-Southerners, the more likely they are to see Northerners as different from themselves, in stereotyped ways.

Similarity is, to some extent, a contrast phenomenon; the presence of a dissimilar third party emphasizes the relative similarity between two others. This means that this sort of identification can be reinforced by an alien context. Differences that seem important within the group may become less so in the presence of "outsiders." For regional groups, this phenomenon may be especially evident among migrants from the region. The differences between Appalachian whites and other white Southerners, for example, seem to be effectively submerged in the cities of the upper Midwest, perhaps partly for this reason. We even have a few testimonials to cases in which black and white Southerners, confronted by hostile or indifferent Northerners, came to realize that they share a cultural heritage.

There is a paradox here, though. The same experiences that heighten this sort of identification—exposure to outsiders, actual or (through education or the media) vicarious—undermine the cultural characteristics on which it is based; the process that brings about awareness of similarity can destroy the similarity itself. This may account for the occasional empirical finding that group identification has little or no correlation with the display of "typical" group characteristics. (There is, for instance, only a slight correlation between segregationist attitudes and regional identification among Southern whites.) Certainly, being or becoming "marginal" can have remarkable results; marginal members of regional groups, like their counterparts in ethnic groups, have often played significant and creative roles in the cultural and political life of their groups.

Presumably, however, there are causal connections between actual similarity, perceived similarity, and identification with the group. Persons who believe themselves to be unlike what they see as the typical member of their group should, in general, identify less strongly with the group. In extreme cases, individuals may identify with the group, or fail to, on grounds of similarity alone. My own research has turned up quite recent migrants to the South who display strong regional identification because they "like the way Southerners do things" or feel "we have a lot in common." I also found lifelong residents who deny that they are Southerners at all because they "don't think that way" or "disagree with Southern attitudes."

The basis of this sort of identification with a regional group is the perception of regional differences. The study of these perceptions is a meeting point for several scholarly disciplines. The prominence in American literature of regional themes (obviously related to the prominence in American letters of identifiably "regional" writers) has ensured the attention of literary scholars to regional "imagery"; American historians have always been concerned with sectional conflict, and some (notably George Tindall) have lately turned to the study of sectional "mythology"; the new field of "cognitive geography" includes among its interests the way people see regional cultures; and some sociologists and social psychologists besides myself have begun, tentatively, to explore regional stereotypes. We know enough (most of it, inevitably, about the South) to know that the subject deserves this attention. To cite just one suggestive example from my own book, *The Enduring South*, a sample of Southern college students ascribed virtually the same list of "most typical traits" to white Northerners and to Americans generally, but saw white Southerners as having little in common with either. (There was, incidentally, more agreement in the choice of typical regional traits than typical racial traits.)

A note may be in order here on the status cues that indicate group membership to others, the most visible "things in common" shared by members of a group. Unlike the stigmata of racial groups, those of American regional groups are not physical. Nor are family names a reliable guide, although they do show regional variation. Wilbur Zelinsky has shown that given names vary by region, too, particularly between the South and the rest of the country, and Southern preferences for "double-barreled" names, diminutives, and suffixes like *Jr.* and *III* have also been documented. But although there are identifiably "Southern" names, the proportion of Southerners who bear them is too small for that to be an accurate indicator. No doubt regional accents are the surest guide, although probably only experts can distinguish much beyond the Southern drawl and perhaps the Appalachian twang.

Regional status cues, then, unlike those of many ethnic groups, are subtle, if not nonexistent. This is made up for in social interaction by the fact that the question "Where are you from?" is regarded as an inoffensive conversation starter. It should be noted, however, that it is relatively easy to acquire or shed a regional identity without risking contradiction from others. This may have some bearing on the transience of regional identity among migrants.

When members of a group can be identified by nonmembers, at least the early stages of interaction will be shaped by whatever stereotypes the nonmembers hold. This can strengthen members' identification in another way. Being treated categorically as a member of the group can lead to a more or less realistic awareness that how one is seen and evaluated by others is dependent on how one's group is perceived. It is not necessary that outsiders' views be derogatory, merely that they appear undiscriminating. And since outsiders are usually less knowledgeable about the group than insiders, their generalizations probably will be seen as undiscriminating, to some extent at least. Peter Gould and Rodney White's study of American college students' regional imagery, in *Mental Maps*, for instance, found that most of the non-Southern students saw the whole South as an unattractive place to live, completely ignoring the distinctions that Southern students drew between Alabama and Mississippi, or North and South Carolina. When outsiders ignore intragroup distinctions, group members may be led to ignore them too—at least when dealing with outsiders. The fact that the distinction between Appalachian and lowland Southern whites is not terribly important among migrants to Midwestern cities may have something to do with the natives' indiscriminate use of the word *hillbilly*.

Being treated categorically, then, can turn a category into a group. This is simply a special case of identification based on perceived interdependence, on the conviction that what is good for the group is good for its members. Interdependence can be based on other things as well, of course: not only members' prestige, but their power or wealth can be seen as linked to that of others in the group. The nature of regional groups, more perhaps than that of other sorts, ensures that this perception is often accurate, since both economic and (in the United States) political organization have, necessarily, a geographical base.

When the collective interests of groups collide, the resulting conflict provides what is probably the classic situation for strengthening group identification, or even for producing a group where none existed before. Conflict notoriously strengthens group solidarity. The extreme case of violent conflict means that not only well-being but life itself can be tied to the group's fortunes, a dramatic sort of interdependence indeed. It should not be surprising that the major regional distinction in the United States—the South *versus* the rest of the country—still reflects the disposition of forces in the nation's most serious sectional conflict. There have, however, been other sectional disputes, with other patterns of alliance. Presumably, these conflicts have either reflected the existence of other regional groups or given rise to such groups.

After all, a common history, perhaps especially a history of conflict, can be the "something in common" on which identification is based. That is why group identification, once established, can exhibit a surprising degree of autonomy, surviving the circumstances that brought it into being. This element of inherited identification is an important point of similarity between regional groups and groups more commonly thought of as ethnic, distinguishing them from other social aggregates that may also have common interests, a common culture, and some measure of group identification (social classes, for example).

Aside from the general proposition that identification based on perceptions of interdependence is heightened by conflict between groups, we know little about the factors that produce it, for individuals or for the group as a whole. It presumably bears some relation to actual interdependence. Groups that are more interdependent—as regional groups may be, by their nature—should show higher levels of identification than others. Within any group, those who actually stand to benefit from improvements in the group's situation should be more likely to believe as much. But we must reckon with the possibility of "false consciousness," here as elsewhere.

In any event, regional identification, on whatever basis, is potentially a significant form of group identification. Certainly, it is significant among white Southerners. A commonly used index incorporating measures of both sorts of identification shows white Southerners to have a level of identification with their regional group higher than that of Roman Catholics with their religious group or that of union members with other unionists. The group identification of Southern whites approaches the levels displayed by blacks and Jews. Group identification is not strongly related to any of the obvious background characteristics, like education, occupation, or urban-rural residence. The importance of family traditions is suggested by the fact that regional identification is strongest among Southerners from the conventionally defined Deep South, weaker among those from Appalachia (largely pro-Union in the Civil War) and more recently settled areas of Florida and the Southwest, and weakest of all among migrants to the South. Some results of a 1971 Survey of North Carolina have similar implications; although substantial majorities of both blacks and Appalachian whites accepted the designation "Southerner" and showed some measure of identification with it, both groups were less likely than other North Carolinians to think of themselves as Southerners at all, and some explicitly rejected the regional label in favor of a national one.

It appears, moreover, that not only regional identification but regional antipathy can be inherited. At least that is one explanation of the finding in *The Enduring South* that anti-Southern sentiment among non-Southerners is strongest in New England and, there, among Republicans.

Regional Cultural Differences

Identification with a regional group can result from cultural differences between one group and another, but it does not *require* such differences. It can be a residual effect of past cultural differences or the result of interdependence based on something else altogether. Regional identification should probably be the criterion for identifying regional groups in the first place, but once they have been identified, an obvious question concerns the nature and extent of the cultural differences among them.

In the past, it went without saying that Westerners were different from New Englanders, and Southerners different from both, and most Americans could say how. Recent evidence on regional stereotyping shows that many still can, whether accurately or not. But it is fair to say that most recent scholarship and reportage on the subject have emphasized the "Americanization" of the nation's hinterlands and implied, at least, that regional cultures were a thing of the past. Perhaps partly as an antiquarian reaction, a few scholars have now begun something like a systematic attempt to see what regional differences remain and whether, in fact, they are disappearing. Their findings may come as a surprise to those who see American society as unfailingly hostile to regional cultures.

Once again, Southerners appear as an extreme case, but one that may serve as a model, suggesting, if nothing else, that regional differences in the United States can be large and important. A 1967 article by Norval Glenn in *Public Opinion Quarterly*, examining a variety of "cultural" questions from a number of national public opinion polls for each of four regions (roughly the same as the census bureau's Northeast, South, Central, and West), confirmed that the South was indeed the most distinctive of the four. (This is not to say that smaller non-Southern regions such as the Mormon West might not be more unusual.) Glenn's subsequent work has shown that differences between white Southerners and other white Americans are far from negligible; they are larger, on the average, than those between urban and rural people, males and females, Protestants and Catholics, or manual and nonmanual workers, and are about the same size, again on the average, as those between blacks and whites. Some of the most obvious and politically significant differences (those in racial attitudes, for instance) have decreased, but despite that, the average difference examined has not decreased in the recent past, may even have increased, and may be larger among young people than among older ones.

The Enduring South also examined selected differences between Southern and non-Southern whites, and found substantial differences in religious beliefs and practices, attitudes toward the family and the local community, and attitudes and behavior involving violence and the private use of force. In general, these differences had not decreased during the generation or so that the study covered, and they could not be explained in any obvious way by regional differences in education, occupation, or rurality.

An examination of how regional cultural differences can come about may suggest why these findings were not expected and also, perhaps, why they should have been. Although it is harder to explain cultural differentiation in a mobile, urban, industrial society like the United States than in a society where more people stay put and where there is no "national" culture or an unobtrusive one, the United States has not been immune to the forces that produce regional cultures in less highly developed societies.

No one maintains, for example, that the United States does not offer a variety of physical environments, and the environment itself has both direct and indirect effects on culture. Climate, terrain, soil, and the like have direct and obvious effects on such things as leisure-time activities, architecture, diet, clothing, and physical health. It is not impossible that the natural "givens" also affect, more subtly, such things as perception and temperament, although we know very little about these matters.

In the early days of the nation, as in all preindustrial societies, the physical data had another momentous effect, determining that different parts of the United States would have different economic bases. Since, according to a variety of sociological theories, how a society makes its living largely determines what sort of culture it has, here is another source of regional differentiation. According to this view, the South, suited for profitable, large-scale, staple crop agriculture, was fated to have a different culture from New England or the Middle West, where climate and soil dictated other economic arrangements. Even if overstated, there is clearly a valuable point here.

Another consequence of economic diversity was a regional division of labor. Partly as a result of that, American regions have not only made their livings differently, some have made better livings than others. The South, for example, was not just an agricultural region, it was a *poor* agricultural region, at least after 1865, and some of the differences between it and the Northeast reflected not the agriculture but the poverty, with all that implies for standard of living, quality of education, public health, and the like.

There is good reason to suppose, however, that most of the cultural effects of regional differences in physical environment are decreasing. Industrialization means that most people in every region now make their livings from occupations dependent on soil and climate only at second or third remove, if that. Urbanization reduces the importance of natural conditions still further. Particularly in the last fifty years, American regions have become more uniformly urban and their occupational structures and average incomes have become more nearly identical. If economic and demographic differences were the only source of cultural differences among regions, the cultural differences should be decreasing as well.

At the same time, advanced technology has made even the direct effects of environment less important. Efficient air conditioning and heating make possible (and other factors make desirable) a national standardization of architecture. Improved transportation and storage work to erode regional differences in diet. North Carolinians ski on artificial snow, while New Yorkers swim in heated pools.

In the United States, however, characterized as it is by relatively late European settlement, there is another possible source of regional cultural differences, besides the effects of environmental variety. Such differences may reflect differences in the regional concentration of immigrant ethnic groups directly, if they merge with the dominant regional groups, as well as indirectly through their effects on other groups in the region. It matters a great deal for the culture of the Northeast, for example, that so much of the late nineteenth- and early twentieth-century immigration went to that region. It matters equally for Southern culture that so little of that immigration went there; and it matters even more that nearly all of the imported Africans did. Similarly, the Mountain States show the influence of the Mormon settlement, while the Latin influence on the Southwest is evident in much more than place names. Many of what are seen as regional differences in the United States may simply be disguised and diffused ethnic differences. Much of what is seen as "Yankee" culture in the South could easily be a New York blend of Irish, Italian, and Jewish contributions, with little input from "old Yankee" culture at all; much of Southern culture may reflect simply the overwhelming preponderance of Evangelical Protestants in the South.

A somewhat less obvious point is that sheer *number* of cultural groups in a region can affect the region's culture, without regard to *which* groups are present. The Northeast has had to adjust to successive waves of newcomers and to the presence of many competing (or at least differing) ethnic groups; its culture perhaps and its politics certainly reflect this fact. The South, on the other hand, has been the arena for two vast racial groups, and there have been virtually no third parties to permit shifting alliances. Both the South and the Northeast *must* differ in important ways from an area characterized by ethnic and religious uniformity.

Of course, settlement patterns are not independent of the natural environment. In the first place, migrants often choose a destination because it allows them to make their livings in accustomed ways, and there are many well-known examples from American immigration history. (We should not forget either that not all migrants have a choice; the requirements of the plantation system account for the geography of black settlement, those of the railroads for that of other groups.) In addition, the derivative effects of natural environment, including its effects on earlier settlement, can attract or repel settlers. The skills of Eastern and Southern European immigrants, for example, were in greater demand in Northern cities than in the plantation society of the South, and in the North they did not have to compete with a black population still in a state of virtual serfdom.

So a region's economic base can affect its ethnic composition. The reverse is also true: economic activity is not completely determined by the physical environment. There is obviously no sponge fishing in Montana, but German settlers in the South, for instance, often continued to operate family farms even after they could afford plantations.

The cultural effects of regional differences in ethnic, religious, or racial composition can be reduced in two ways: if the regional differences in composition are themselves reduced, or if the cultural differences among ethnic, religious, and racial groups decrease. Both of these processes may be occurring—the first through migration, the second through acculturation—but they are proceeding very slowly and erratically, and apparently not at all for some groups. Regional cultural differences based on these factors will presumably be more durable than those based on regional economic differences.

So long as economic and demographic differences exist among American regions, those differences will produce not only the obvious sort of cultural effects we have been considering, but indirect, "contextual" effects as well. A place gives its inhabitants not only a physical environment but a social and cultural one. The religious contexts of the Northeast and the South, for example, are quite different, and must have cultural effects even on those who do not share their regions' major religions. Southerners have not only been likely to be poor themselves, they have lived among poor people. The second-order effects of regional differences in economy and demography will decrease with the latter, but, as we observed, some of the latter are not decreasing.

When regional populations can be regarded as *groups*, a rather different view of their subcultures emerges, and perhaps an even greater estimate of their hardiness. A group can be said to have had "collective experiences," and some aspects of its culture may be responses to those experiences. It seems at least possible, for example, that the culture of the West includes some legacies from the frontier experience, and several treatments of Southern culture have seen much of it as an adaptation to the threatened and vulnerable position of the South in the antebellum period.

Cultural characteristics of this sort can be sustained by current, analogous experiences at either the group or the individual level. If Southern culture is partly an adaptation to external threat, its vitality has no doubt been reinforced by continuing attacks on the "Southern way of life." (Not that many Southerners must feel threatened much of the time, merely enough to keep the consequent responses "at large" in the subculture, where the normal mechanisms of socialization can ensure that they are shared by the unthreatened as well.) Similarly, if the West's subculture reflects the experience of uprooting and migration, the associated cultural themes can be kept prominent by the continuing arrival of new migrants.

If we can think of a group per se as having experiences, it follows that individuals who identify with the group can feel that these experiences are somehow their own, and the cultural consequences of these experiences can be found in persons who have not themselves had even analogous experiences. There is evidence, for example, that the rejection by Congress of two Southern nominees to the Supreme Court was seen by many white Southerners as an affront to the region, and thus indirectly to themselves. Whatever the cultural consequences of rejection, they were presumably reinforced by this vicarious "experience."

In the extreme case, living members of the group can undergo the experience *only* vicariously, because it is in the remote past, or even fictitious. Another view of Southern culture, of which C. Vann Woodward's is the best-known formulation, sees it not so much as a defensive adaptation as a response to the historical experience of defeat, frustration, and subordination. But no less important than the historical reality is the question of how that history is presented to Southerners today. Like any other group, a regional group has a myth of itself that furnishes not only a basis for identification but a rationale for at least some aspects of its culture. Understanding that myth may be the key to understanding not only how members feel toward their group but how they think and feel about a great deal else.

Institutions and Regional Culture

A regional culture, like any other, is shaped and transmitted by institutions—by the family, the school, the church, the press, political and voluntary organizations, and the like. Members of the regional group not only learn appropriate ways to feel and behave, but they learn that the group exists and something of its situation. Unfortunately, in the case of regional groups, little is known about how these lessons are taught or the institutions that do the teaching.

The obvious place to start is with institutions that are explicitly regional, those that claim to speak for or to serve the members of some regional group, though genuine examples of such organizations are rare. There is no shortage of organizations and associations with terms like *Midwestern* or *Southern* in their titles, to be sure, but undoubtedly the majority of these are specialized, functional bodies, having more to do with physical location or, at most, geographically based common problems than with a regional group of any sort. Regional professional associations, regional airlines and railways, college athletic conferences, and the like may be in the region but not of it—although the comparative study of such organizations might reveal some unexpected regional emphases. Similarly, governors' conferences, regional boards and commissions, and other interstate political arrangements typically exist to deal with problems that transcend state boundaries. Sometimes they articulate sectional interests based on those problems and become involved in sectional conflict, but in general their relation to any "ethnic" region is marginal, at best (although occasionally the relation is stronger than the organization desires: the letterhead of the Southern Growth Policies Board includes Delaware, Maryland, and Texas in its map of the South, for instance, but all three states have so far declined invitations to subscribe). Aside from acknowledging the existence of a region, and encouraging people to think of it as somehow a fact of nature, the role of most regional organizations in the group life of American regional groups seems to be minimal.

Occasionally, however, regional groups have spawned organizations devoted to preserving some version of their culture or propagating some myth of their experience. Sometimes these organizations have claimed to speak for the group as a whole, or at least for all "authentic" members of it, but they have, as a rule, been so unrepresentative of the regional group that their claims should be viewed with some skepticism. The Mayflower Society, for instance, or the United Daughters of the Confederacy is intentionally exclusive—too much so to be typical of its region. Still, the role of such societies deserves more attention than it has received. Just as the Ku Klux Klan in its several incarnations has displayed some instructive similarities to various ethnic "defense" organizations (and evoked some of the same ambivalence among those whose culture was supposedly being defended), the genealogically based, filiopietistic organization is found in many groups other than regional ones.

Another institution that deserves attention as a medium for regional culture is the contemporary regional press. (Indeed, it is significant that there is one, and that it is flourishing.) Month after month, such magazines as *Yankee, Sunset, Southern Living,* and *New York* tell their readers what it means to be a New Englander, Westerner, Southerner, or New Yorker. The message is largely subliminal, conveyed as much by advertising as by editorial content, but it is there. Certainly, only part of the regional group (generally the upper-middle class) is being addressed; even so, the analogy to the ethnic press is close.

But explicitly regional institutions in the United States do tend to be uninteresting, from the point of view of someone interested in regional identity and culture. There are, however, a number of quasi-regional institutions that demand attention. Perhaps the most significant are regionally based churches and Protestant denominations. It is impossible to deny the uniquely influential position of the Mormon church in the Mountain States, for example, or that of the Southern Baptist Convention in the South.

The latter began—as its name indicates—as an explicitly Southern church, separating itself from the "American" Baptists during the antebellum slavery controversy. (There were parallel developments in other denominations.) It served for some time as essentially an ethnic church, following its members in their migration to the North and West, but was otherwise concentrated in the South. Although now well on the way to becoming a national—indeed, international—denomination, the Southern Baptists retain their dominance in the life of the South; nearly half the population identify themselves as Baptists, and even that figure probably understates Baptist influence in the region. Heretofore, the relation of the Southern Baptist Convention to its region of origin has been pretty much taken for granted, but as the denomination is "de-ethnicized," perhaps some attention will now be given to how it has worked to shape and to reinforce Southern culture, both in Southern communities and among migrants from the region.

Here again the South may present the clearest case, this time of a regional group with a distinctive religious orientation, expressed in its case through the Baptist and other Evangelical Protestant churches. It is difficult to identify other churches as regional, in the sense that Congregationalism used to be identified with New England. Migration and missionary activity have had consequences both for the regional composition of American religious groups and for the religious composition of American regional groups. Nevertheless, most religious groups in

America are still regionally concentrated, religious and regional affilia-
tion are correlated, religious controversy has often expressed itself as
sectional conflict, and the contributions of religious bodies to the life of
American regional groups and to American regional cultures need to
be investigated.

Another quasi-regional institution that deserves attention is the de
facto regional university—a state or private institution that serves, in
effect, to educate a regional elite or functions as a center for regional
scholarship. Although the University of the South at Sewanee, Tennessee, never fulfilled its founders' ambitions for it, there was a time when
the University of North Carolina served that purpose for the South, to
a great extent, and it may be that Stanford still does the same for the
West. Studies of where these institutions recruited their students,
where they placed their graduates, and their relation to the major national universities could tell us something about regional, and national,
leadership. Universities' roles in interpreting regional cultures also
need to be examined; it is still the case, for example, that courses in
the history, culture, and social structure of the South are offered in at
least seven departments of the University of North Carolina at Chapel
Hill.

Other examples of quasi-regional institutions could be discussed, but
since they have seldom been examined in that light, we know even
less about them than about regional churches and universities. In any
event, the major agencies for transmitting the self-images and subcultures of American regional groups are not themselves regional or
quasi-regional but exist instead at the level of local communities.

Since New England communities are usually dominated by New Englanders and Southern communities by Southerners, the ordinary
community institutions can serve the cultural purposes of the regional
group unobtrusively, and they are seldom seen as "regional"—much
less "ethnic"—at all. Although one study of the daily press found regional variation in the style, emphasis, and implicit values of its news
coverage, for example, the local newspaper is not usually regarded as
an ethnic organ. Although the teaching of national religious denominations has been shown to vary at the congregational level from region
to region, local churches are seldom seen as ethnic churches. State and
local history courses may serve the same functions for regional cultures
as ethnic studies courses for other cultures, but their presence in the

public schools has long been taken for granted. The importance of family traditions has already been indicated, and the transmission of regional culture and identity within families is even less open to casual observation.

This symbiotic relation between regional culture and local institutions is most obvious in the case of the South. Probably its effects on journalism, religion, and education are most obvious there simply because Southern culture is the most distinctive of America's regional variants. The same processes at work in other regions may just produce results that most observers find less remarkable.

The fact that ordinary local institutions can serve the needs of the regional group may account, in part, for the relative absence of explicitly regional institutions. Unlike ethnic groups in more heterogeneous situations, regional groups will not usually need to establish an array of parallel institutions for their members. Sometimes, however, the cultural role of local institutions is brought into sharp relief, sometimes even threatened, by the arrival (physical or political) of unsympathetic "outsiders" who object to the use of community facilities to promote a culture and world view they do not share. In some Southern states, for example, newly arrived Northerners and newly enfranchised blacks have joined to attack the view of the Southern past presented by state history textbooks. In some communities, the Southern white response has been to withdraw to private "segregation academies," where their cultural hegemony can be preserved. These schools (often under the unlikely auspices of Protestant churches whose hostility to parochial education was formerly unrelenting) are devoted to preserving a version of white Southern culture that includes a good deal more than just white supremacist ideology, but they do represent one answer to the question of whether the regional group can be taken to include Southern blacks.

Although regional cultures may sometimes be challenged on their home ground, the greatest need for cultural support from parallel institutions is clearly where the analogy between regional groups and immigrant ethnic groups is closest, that is, among enclaves of migrants from the home region. Although there has been some attention to the situation of Southern migrants to the upper Midwest, as in Lewis Killian's *White Southerners*, we know very little about the California confraternities based on state of origin, for example, or about upper-middle-class executives and managers who have followed their industries from the Northeast to the South and Southwest. Systematic study of migrants could tell us how they sustain their group life, when, in fact, they do. It could also help us understand the circumstances under which regional identity and regional cultural emphases persist outside the region, when they are passed on to later generations, and what role regional identity plays in social interaction—whether, for instance, it has anything to do with the choice of a marriage partner.

Looking at regional populations as groups obviously raises more questions than we now have answers for. It not only raises new questions but puts old ones in a new light. Occupational specialization is a frequent characteristic of immigrant groups, for example. When we find Southerners overrepresented in the military (as, apparently, they always have been), are we seeing the same sort of phenomenon? We know in what circles John Kennedy's religious background was a political liability, but who held Jimmy Carter's origins against him? Crime rates are known to vary from one ethnic group to another, a fact that has led to some productive theorizing. The South's homicide rate has received some attention, but has no one noticed that the West's rape rate is equally remarkable? Do we need separate explanations for the dominance in twentieth-century American literature of Southerners and Jews? "The Nashville Sound" is not the only ethnic contribution to mass popular culture. What does such widespread acceptance tell us about the status of the group from which it comes? These and many other questions follow immediately from applying the categories and procedures from the study of ethnicity to the investigation of regional groups. Only when the questions are answered will we be able to say how close an analogy there is, but it is obviously close enough to merit attention.

2. Whatever Became of Regional Sociology?

As recently as mid-century, the sociological study of American regions seemed to be in vigorous good health. An impressive symposium published in 1951, *Regionalism in America*, included contributions from two sociologists: Howard W. Odum, the founder of a tradition he called "regional sociology," and Rupert B. Vance, Odum's most distinguished student. In 1952, Odum's journal, *Social Forces*, published an article, "Regional Sociology as a Special Discipline," celebrating the subfield's accomplishments, outlining areas for further investigation, and displaying no intimations of mortality. Over the previous twenty years, Odum, his students and colleagues at the University of North Carolina, and other American sociologists (most of them, to be sure, at Southern institutions) had produced a vast and apparently enduring body of work on regional variation in the United States—work that, to all appearances, had established a legitimate school within American sociology and claimed a place for sociologists as equal partners in the cross-disciplinary enterprise of regional studies.

Twenty years later, however, regional sociology, at least in its application to the major regions of the United States, had sunk without a trace. The American Sociological Association listed sixty-four specialities for its members to identify themselves with, but regional study was not among them. Articles were not being published on the subject, even in *Social Forces*; papers were not being read, even at meetings of the Southern Sociological Society. The University of North Carolina continued to offer a course entitled Regional Sociology of the South, but it was, to my knowledge, the only course on American regional studies to be offered in any American sociology department, and it was open only to undergraduates. A 1973 article by Frank Westie in *The American Sociologist* reported that nearly half of a sample of young sociology Ph.D.'s, asked to identify former presidents of the American Sociological Association, confessed that they had never heard of Howard Odum, and another third said the name was familiar, but they did not know his work. The concerns of the early regional sociologists continued to be addressed, but by planners, geographers, anthropologists, and students of "regional science" (an outgrowth of regional economics), not by sociologists. Within American sociology, only the semi-autonomous subfields of human ecology and rural sociology showed any trace of an intellectual debt to regional sociology, and their concerns were with smaller, and perhaps more manageable, "regions"— river valleys, metropolitan areas, and the like—not great historic sections like New England, the Midwest, or the South.

Why this abrupt turn for the worse in what seemed to be a flourishing subdiscipline? Why has regional sociology bequeathed so little to American sociology in general? Are there signs of a renewed interest in American regionalism among sociologists in the United States, and, if so, what is the relation of the new interest to the old?

With hindsight, it is possible to say that whatever else it may have been, regional sociology was not very good *sociology*. It failed to use sociological criteria for problem finding; it was not satisfactorily anchored in modern sociological theory; and the political context in which Odum and his students worked directed their attention to some transitory, if important, problems, and away from what can be seen in retrospect as more enduring aspects of American regionalism. In the 1950s, Odum died and other principal figures in the movement retired or turned to other interests; the South's economic and social problems, a central concern of many regional sociologists, appeared on the way to being solved; and the study of conflict-generating divisions within American society (which regional sociology manifestly was, despite Odum's unceasing protests to the contrary) became unfashionable. Faced with these developments, and given its uncertain foundations, regional sociology barely survived its founder.

The tenuous relation of regional sociology to its parent discipline is evident even in what regional sociologists chose to call their undertaking—sometimes regional sociology, sometimes "regionalism" (an all-purpose word referring also to Odum's ideology of regional balance and integration). By whatever name, the field had an ambitious program. One aspect of it, Alvin Bertrand wrote in *Social Forces*, was "the study of all forms of human association within the regional environment." Rupert Vance went still further; the goal, he said, was "to show the region as a totality." And Svend Riemer announced, "With the coordination of technology, biology, geography, economy, and sociology, regionalism establishes itself as a new superscience."

As is often the case with such holistic approaches, however, the study of *all* turned out in practice to mean the study of *everything*. One has to wonder what many of the early titles in regional sociology have to do with sociology, while other titles, clearly sociological, have nothing specifically regional about them. They are, to borrow a useful distinction from Edgar Thompson, sociology in, not of, a region. The envisioned synthesis was never to be; the preliminary analysis was never complete. And, indeed, it probably never could be. Some selection must be exercised, some data discarded as irrelevant. The existing academic disciplines give sensible, or at least explicit and time-honored, answers to the question of *which*. (Vance seems to have believed that the restriction of focus to a single geographical area does the same, but to understand a region "as a totality" is only marginally less difficult than to do the same for a nation—or the world.) A less enthusiastic approach, asking what is *sociologically* interesting about a region or about the regional structure of a nation, would not have been foredoomed to failure.

Such an approach would also have required that more attention be paid to the theoretical underpinnings of regional sociology. In 1943, Rudolf Heberle, in a *Social Forces* article called "Regionalism: Some Critical Observations," observed that despite some fine empirical research and significant advances in methodology, the regionalists were neither drawing on nor contributing to the developing body of general sociological theory, and this isolation continued to characterize the field. Odum did attempt to fill the theoretical void with what he called "folk-regional sociology," but the conclusion is regrettably unavoidable that this was an unfortunate development. An unstable and eclectic compound of neo-Hegelianism and conservative Social Darwinism, folk-regional theory was unsound and, perhaps worse, old-fashioned. It is difficult to believe that anyone beyond the circle of Odum's students ever took the trouble to penetrate his cumbersome prose to figure out what he was saying; certainly few others ever cited his theoretical contributions. Perhaps the most telling criticism of folk-regional theory is that it failed the test of practice; the theory had few discernible effects on the research of Odum's colleagues or even on Odum's own. Looking back, in a 1960 *Journal of Southern History* symposium, Rupert Vance remarked that regional sociologists were "much better at taking in other people's washing, relating [their] contributions to those of geography, economics, political science, and so forth than . . . in relating regionalism to its own domain, that of general sociology." Since nothing in the intellectual patrimony of American "general sociology" obliged it to take regionalism seriously, any connection would have to have been made by the regionalists. But folk-regional theory, essentially an autonomous development, failed to bridge the gap. Sociologists outside the regional sociology "school" were given no reason to suppose that the activities of the regionalists were related to their own interests and concerns.

Finally, in addition to its immodest goals and modest theoretical base, regional sociology suffered from a politically induced distortion of its activities. On one hand, Odum and his colleagues wished to get into politics, to the extent of planning for regional development—in particular, for most of them, for the economic development of the South. On the other hand, they wished to stay *out* of politics, by not inflaming sectional feeling or furnishing ammunition for the Southern politicians they usually referred to as demagogues. This desire and this apprehension—the intent to do sociology *for*, as well as *of* and *in*, the South—led to a neglect of subjects not seen as problems, and of problems not seen as amenable to political solution. In their research, Odum and his colleagues displayed an almost single-minded attention to regional differences in wealth, occupational structure, and standard of living. In their concern to avoid "sectionalism" (the illegitimate sibling of "regionalism," in Odum's view), they disregarded elements in Southern culture that probably had historical rather than economic or demographic roots, and largely ignored the perplexing subject of regional identity or regional consciousness. At times one catches a glimpse of a naïvely materialistic view that sees all cultural differences as epiphenomena of economic differences (as some were, of course) and sees regional identity, if at all, as based solely on common interests stemming from these economic differences.

Again and again, critics of regional sociology remarked this shortcoming. In 1940, J. O. Hertzler observed in *Social Forces* that "it may be said quite truthfully that the regionalists have not explored the social psychological aspects of their subject" and called for the study of regional influences on "sentiments, wishes, interests . . . loyalties, attitudes and thought patterns." Three years later, Heberle produced a similar catalog of deficiencies, and urged in particular "the uncovering of the bases for [regional] sentiment and the analysis of the socio-psychological nature of this regional 'consciousness of kind' and its bearing upon the social groupings and processes in the region." He attacked the materialist position directly. "People in a region, if this is a genuine social entity at all, are likely to be 'bound' not merely by 'common interest,' but, much more important, are often the imponderable factors of a common tradition and history. Such ties may be much more lasting and forceful than those based on mere interest." In 1945, Walter Kollmorgen pointed out, in the *American Economic Review*, the theoretical importance of "psychic [cultural] homogeneity and difference" in the study of regions and argued that "these qualities present legitimate fields of inquiry for research workers." "Unfortunately," he observed, "the mounting literature on regionalism neglects this field almost entirely." A few years later, Bertrand could still observe that "research into the social-psychological aspects of regional aggregates would be of much use and represents [an] area in which stress is needed."

In fact, Odum himself did not neglect such questions. In a number of works devoted to what he called regional "portraiture," he discussed such matters at length and underlined the point with his emphasis in his theoretical works on regional "folkways" and "folk consciousness." He even pointed to the importance of such factors in the process of regional delineation, remarking once, for instance, that a region *is* "an area of which the inhabitants feel themselves a part." But this work, when not "theoretical," was qualitative, subjective, and essentially impressionistic. When Odum turned to more empirical work, in *Southern Regions of the United States*, he defined the South, not on the basis of how Southerners felt about it, but by examining over seven hundred more "objective" indicators, most of them related to agriculture, rurality, and poverty. One anomalous result was that Texas was excluded. (It is amusing to note in the official history of the Southern Sociological Society that figures for attendance, by state, at the society's meetings show large numbers of conventioneers from "other," non-Southern states for the first several years—until someone evidently decided that Texans were going to continue to define themselves as Southerners after all, and started to count them separately.) In *Southern Regions*, Odum revealed the conflicting demands of theory and practice when discussing the case of Maryland: "To attempt to characterize or plan for Maryland as a region of farm tenancy or of Negro-white population or of agrarian culture or of children per 1,000 women or of . . . a hundred other socio-economic factors, basic to needs and planning, was at once to invalidate the scientific validity of regional analysis. On the other hand, to add Maryland's aggregate to the Southeast in the effort to bolster up [the Southeast's] claims and ratings would defeat the object of reaching working differentials upon which to reach accurate diagnosis." For these purposes, if Marylanders feel themselves a part of the South, they are simply mistaken; they are not poor enough, rural enough, fertile enough, and so on through the "hundred other socio-economic factors."

Is it surprising, given the "problem" orientation of the regionalists and the training of their students, that, in time, many should have felt that their subject matter was disappearing? "Many of the basic conditions that gave rise to regional disability and differences have simply evaporated on our doorsteps," Vance wrote in 1960. "The New Deal has been dealt. . . . As the affluent society crosses the Mason-Dixon line, the regionalist of the 1930s turns up as just another 'liberal without a cause.'" Vance's interests, like those of other regionalists, turned increasingly to the problems of the Third World, which on the surface, at least, were like those of the South in the 1920s and 1930s, and to the Appalachian region of the United States, largely bypassed by the South's economic development.

Regional sociology never really produced a third generation. Those who studied with the second generation have pursued careers, and sometimes achieved distinction, in demography, human ecology, the study of modernization and development, rural sociology, and elsewhere. But, as a school and as a movement, regionalism succumbed to the loss of its leaders, who had somehow held it all together, to an emerging consensus on what "general sociology" was (a consensus the regionalists had not really contributed to, and which excluded them), and to the solution of some of the most pressing of the practical problems that had inspired the movement in the first place.

And there matters remained for some years. Not only regional sociology, but any sort of sociological interest in regions of the United States (other than the Appalachians) was hard to find during the 1950s and 1960s. Since 1970 or so, however, some interesting things have been happening, and it may not be premature to speak of a modest revival, if not a full-fledged renaissance.

In the first place, a number of sociologists from a variety of backgrounds, with little in common with one another and probably less in common with the older regionalists, more or less independently returned to the study of regional variation in the United States. When I began at Columbia University in the late sixties the research later published as *The Enduring South*, it would not be exaggerating a great deal to say that my interests were seen as eccentric, if harmless. But at about the same time, Norval Glenn, at the University of Texas, began to write some disturbing articles suggesting that regional cultural differences in the United States remained quite large, were not decreasing as rapidly as everyone assumed, and, indeed, might not be decreasing at all. And Lewis Killian, a Georgian teaching at the University of Massachusetts, published a book, *White Southerners*, that also challenged the conventional view that American regional groups were sinking into the national mainstream. Not too much later, Raymond Gastil, a researcher in Seattle, published a similar article, later incorporated in his book *Cultural Regions of the United States*. I want to emphasize that all this activity was independent. There has not been, and is not now, anything like a school—not even an "invisible college." If there is a common thread, it is that all of us take seriously a point Heberle made in 1943: that the most interesting thing about a region sociologically is that it may contain or give rise to a regional *group*, and we are engaged in studying those groups and their cultures. (It is also worth mentioning that all four think of themselves first as sociologists, not regionalists, and that each has published on other sociological subjects.)

A related development has been that a number of sociological works that a decade or two earlier would have been presented as studies rather inadvertently *in* some region have unabashedly emphasized their regional implications and border on the sociology *of* a region. Where we once had Floyd Hunter's *Community Power Structure*, conducted in Atlanta but suggesting that its findings applied to American (perhaps Western) cities in general, we now see works like Chandler Davidson's *Biracial Politics* and Dwight Billings' *Planters and the Making of a "New South,"* works that emphasize, indeed depend upon, their regional setting. This may be merely an instance of the more general rehabilitation of the case study in American sociology. There is now, it seems to me, less insistence on the fiction that we are studying processes abstracted from time and space.

Finally, there has been some activity on another, but complementary, front. A 1976 article by David Walls, "Central Appalachia: A Peripheral Region Within an Advanced Capitalist Society," in the *Journal of Sociology and Social Welfare*, can stand as an example of the application to the United States of a form of analysis being reintroduced in American sociology, notably by Immanuel Wallerstein. The study of "political economy" was not unknown in the older regional sociology; Edgar Thompson's studies of the plantation and some of Vance's early work on the South's colonial economy (his phrase) led directly into it, but it was largely abandoned by the regionalists as lending aid and comfort to sectionalism, and it was out of fashion for some time in American sociology generally. It has come back now, with a vengeance, and it is good to see that the internal structure of the United States is not being ignored.

This renewal of sociological interest in the regions of the United States is reflected, for instance, in the programs of professional association meetings. The Southern Sociological Society once again has sessions on regional sociology, the sociology of the South, or, often, both. The Mid-South Sociological Association also routinely schedules such sessions and has, in fact, devoted an entire yearly meeting to the sociology of the South. As usual, the South leads in the self-consciousness sweeps, but the Pacific Sociological Association has also devoted a session to regional sociology (although I must note that the session organizer was an expatriate Texan, and the session included papers from a Southerner and a Canadian, both more accustomed to regional analysis than their West Coast hosts).

There has also been a proliferation of courses offered by sociology departments on regional topics, most of them, inevitably, on the sociology of the South. Aside from a dozen or so in Southern institutions, I can cite courses in Boston; Lawrence, Kansas; and Walla Walla, Washington. (Why those places have not cast down their buckets where they are remains a mystery to me. Can it be that the South is simply more *interesting* than New England, the Midwest, or the Pacific Northwest?)

In any case, we can—and should—ask how this new interest in American regions has come about. It seems to me that there are two reasons for it. In the first place, there is the sheer obstinacy of the facts. Again and again, the "regional factor" arises to complicate the inquiries of those interested in other things altogether. N. J. Demerath, for example, in his fine study *Social Class in American Protestantism*, remarks offhandedly that he has excluded Southerners from his sample because these things work differently for them. In *The Religious Factor*, based on data from Detroit, Gerhard Lenski excluded Southern-born respondents for the same reason. In *The Professional Soldier*, Morris Janowitz observes that a striking proportion of the professional officer corps are Southerners or have Southern ties through marriage or education, but he is at something of a loss to explain the fact. Obviously, things work differently for Southerners there, too.

There are a great many regional differences that the early regionalists never got around to examining—differences that are still around and that sooner or later would attract attention. Neglecting the effects of regional environment usually means a lot of "unexplained variance." Social psychologists interested in personal identity might wish it otherwise, but it is a fact that white Southerners display a level of identification with their group that exceeds that of American Roman Catholics and trade union members and approaches that of blacks and Jews. When survey researchers find in region a variable that makes more difference in responses, on the average, than occupation does, more than religion does, more than urban-rural residence does, as much as race and probably as much as education does (all these are Norval Glenn's findings), when they find a variable like that, how much longer can they treat it as a nuisance and pass it off with *ad hoc* explanations? There are substantial regional differences in most of the things sociologists are interested in—urban ecology; homicide, suicide, burglary, and rape rates; child-rearing practices, race relations, and religious beliefs; labor relations, social mobility, and political attitudes—and most of these differences are not decreasing. The merely empirical case for studying them is impressive, if not compelling.

A second reason for the revival, I think, is that American sociology is not isolated from the currents and tides affecting intellectual life generally. Readers hardly need to be reminded of the centrifugal tendencies lately evident in many industrial countries and of the scholarly attention they have received. If sectionalism in the United States, chronic rather than acute and not at present overlaid with nationalist politics, is a pale reflection of similar phenomena in Europe and Canada, perhaps the renewed sociological attention to it can be seen as an even paler reflection of our European and Canadian colleagues' interests. It seems to me, however, that it is best viewed more parochially, as a development related to the renewed interest in ethnicity and race in the United States, beginning in the late 1960s. As blacks began to demand, and receive, more attention from the American academy, it was natural that other groups should press their claims—first, American Indians and the immigrant ethnic groups, then other groups, less obviously ethnic. In the case of white Southerners, the analogy was often quite conscious. Killian's *White Southerners* was published in a series called Ethnic Groups in American Life, and *The Enduring South* argued that the concept of ethnicity was the key to the study of the questions of culture and identity that had eluded the early regionalists. By and large, students of American ethnicity have welcomed regional groups on board the ethnic bandwagon. In *Ethnicity in the United States*, Andrew Greeley devoted a chapter to the subject of regional variation, and the editors of the *Harvard Encyclopedia of American Ethnic Groups* commissioned entries on Southerners, Appalachian whites, and (presumably for balance) Yankees.

What does the work of the regional sociologists have to contribute, besides an instructive example, to those undertaking similar tasks today? Alvin Bertrand listed two other activities of the regionalists besides "the study of all forms of human association": the not-so-simple business of delineating regions and "the comparative study of regional social systems." In both areas they made contributions that are still valuable. Part of the regionalist legacy to geographers was some notable early advances in conceptual clarification and in the methodology of regional definition; they were among the first, for instance, to apply factor analysis to that task. In that respect, recent work in the sociology of American regions has regressed; we tend to take our regions, or at least our techniques for defining them, from geographers, and rather uncritically at that. While this may be a useful—and it is certainly an obvious—division of labor, it is pleasant for sociologists to reflect that the disciplinary balance of trade has not always been one-sided.

It is in the comparative study of regional social systems, however, that the regionalist contribution will prove most enduring, I believe. When the regionalists were at their least ambitious, they produced a flood of remarkable descriptive material, most of it on the South, which will provide a base line for studies of continuity and change for years to come. This work—consciously or not—was organized by a principle of selection, the comparative method, which emphasizes regional differences, neglecting those things (and there are many) which American regions have in common. I think this lowering of sights, abandoning the attempt to describe "the region as a totality," is the key to a successful regional sociology—and it certainly marks the most successful work of the early regionalists. David Potter, a distinguished historian of the South, suggests that a similar restriction might be useful for regional studies in other disciplines as well. Southern studies, he wrote, "should not be concerned indiscriminately with everything that occurs within the South: rather they should focus their analysis at points where the conditions of the Southern region differ from those of other regions and should concentrate their attention upon . . . developments which are relevant to these differences. The student is dealing with an entity—the South—whose boundaries are indeterminate, whose degree of separateness has fluctuated historically over time, whose distinctiveness may be in some respects fictitious. His job in this complex of uncertainties is to identify and investigate the distinctive features of Southern society." If Potter is right, obviously his observations apply to the study of any region. We need, in other words, to keep in mind the differences among studies in, of, and for a region.

I have indicated what I believe to be some of the strengths of the modest comeback of regional studies in American sociology. In closing, let me mention two weaknesses. The impulse to study sectionalism may be, like its subject matter, a sign of localism (not to say that word's derogatory synonyms). In any case, the recent sociological work on American regions, like the earlier, has been largely a matter of Southerners studying the South (almost entirely so, if Appalachia is included in the South). Whether from modesty or lack of interest, few of the sociologists involved in this revival have paid much attention to regional variation outside the South. Most deal, at least by implication, with their region in contrast to an amorphous, undifferentiated non-South, which comprises all the rest of the United States from Hawaii to Maine. To be sure, the South is the most peculiar and self-conscious major region in the United States, but some of the others have their own noteworthy features, and the West, in particular, certainly deserves a regional sociologist's attention.

Another sign of our localism is one we share with much of American sociology: I refer to sheer ignorance of related work outside the United States. The persistence of sectionalism in the United States is, as I suggested above, paralleled by the regional and ethnic nationalisms now troubling many Western states (and not just Western ones, for that matter). As a group, those sociologists who have been writing about the American South are remarkably well read in American geography, in Southern history and literary studies, and in the other social sciences' sometimes extensive literature on their region; but from their published writings there is little evidence that any of them are acquainted with even the sociological literature on British, Spanish, French, or even Canadian regionalism. Now that we have put Odum's phobia concerning sectionalism behind us and recognize that such sentiments are very near the heart of the matter, it may be that we are ready to introduce a comparative dimension of a different sort into our work, and in that way to make our work of more than regional interest.

3. Max Weber's Relatives and Other Distractions
Southerners and Sociology

One of the ways the South has differed from the rest of the United States is in the ways its distinguished sons and daughters attain distinction. In a 1939 *Social Forces* article, Rupert Vance examined the *Dictionary of American Biography* from a regionalist's viewpoint and observed that the South seemed to specialize in producing outstanding soldiers, lawyers, and politicians. It was much less likely than the rest of the country, it appeared, to bring forth distinguished scholars, businessmen, or artists. Recently, Janice Coulter took a look at *Who's Who in America* to see whether those patterns still hold up. She found that, by and large, they do, although the South also produces relatively large numbers of outstanding athletes and entertainers, categories not heavily represented in the *DAB*, and clergymen.

So there has been and still is something of a regional division of labor in the United States, and here I want to examine one aspect of it, namely, regional specialization in intellectual pursuits. In particular, I want to ask why the South has produced so few outstanding sociologists. Let me say at the outset that this essay is exploratory—a way of saying that I don't have much in the way of data to work with, merely some impressions, some speculations, and some hunches that don't even deserve to be called hypotheses.

I recognize that a shortage of sociologists, even a shortage of *good* sociologists, is not the most pressing problem the South faces today, and no doubt many Southerners have never even realized that this particular deficiency exists. But it does, nevertheless. There have been many distinguished Southern sociologists, don't misunderstand me. (Rupert Vance was outstanding among them.) But among really first-rate American sociologists, Southerners are much rarer than the 25 to 30 percent one would expect if region of origin had nothing to do with the matter. Only one of the top dozen or so departments of sociology in the country is located at a Southern institution; since that one is my own, I can report with authority that, with a generous definition, only three of its twenty-five faculty members could be regarded as Southerners. I forget how long it has been since a Southerner was president of the American Sociological Association—Rupert Vance may have been the last.

Of course, sociology is not the only academic field in which Southerners do not shine. In most areas, the South has not contributed its share to the intellectual luster of the United States in this century. Whatever your measure—Nobel Prizes, distinguished graduate departments, presidents of scholarly associations, fellows of various academies, authors of prize-winning monographs—whatever your measure, the South comes up short. Partly, of course, this is simply a matter of money. There was a time, not long ago, when the endowments of Harvard and Yale exceeded those of all Southern colleges and universities combined, and a region with a per capita income 60 percent of the national average—like the South of the 1930s—cannot be expected to have its share of expensive luxuries, which is what scholars sometimes appear to be.

But the fact is that some intellectual pursuits have fared better than others in the South. We come a lot closer to holding our own in the professions, for instance, especially in medicine and law. In the liberal arts, I think we have at least our share of first-rate historians, writers, and literary critics. The South is weakest in the natural and social sciences. I will treat sociology because I know it best, but what I have to say may apply to the other sciences as well. If the shoe fits, economists, psychologists, and physicists can lace it for themselves.

Let me sketch the history of sociology in the South. The discipline's connection with the region goes way back, back to 1854 in fact, when George Fitzhugh of Virginia and Henry Hughes of Mississippi almost simultaneously published books with the newfangled Greco-Latin hybrid word *sociology* in their titles. These were the first American titles to use the word, which had been coined a few decades earlier by the French philosopher, Auguste Comte (with whom, as a matter of fact, Henry Hughes had studied in Paris).

Unfortunately for the history of sociology in America, both Fitzhugh's *Sociology for the South* and Hughes's *Treatise on Sociology* were "sociological" defenses of the peculiar Southern institution. With the demise of chattel slavery came the demise, intellectually speaking, of its defenders; Fitzhugh and Hughes, remembered today only by historians, turned out to be not so much the fathers of American sociology as something on the order of bachelor uncles who died without heirs.

The closing years of the nineteenth century saw the reimportation of sociology from Europe, lodging this time in the more hospitable soil of New England, the Middle West, and New York (where the first chair of sociology, so named, was established in 1894 at Columbia University and occupied by Franklin Giddings). Sociology as an academic enterprise didn't make much headway in the South until the 1920s.[1] It was then that Howard Odum, a Georgian who had studied with Giddings at Columbia, founded the South's first sociology department at the University of North Carolina, and he quickly set up all the apparatus of a modern social science establishment as well: a journal (*Social Forces*), a research bureau (the Institute for Research in Social Science), and a half-dozen other supporting institutions, all of them still flourishing. (In these undertakings, it should be noted, he had the support and encouragement of Northern philanthropy and of Northern scholars, especially his former teacher, Giddings.) At about the same time, other Southerners who had gone North to study sociology began to return: Edgar Thompson, from South Carolina to the University of Chicago to Duke; William Cole, from Tennessee to Cornell and back to the University of Tennessee; and a dozen others. Many who went North to study never did come back, or at least not until they were ready to retire; but enough returned, and they subsequently trained enough students, for the Southern Sociological Society to be founded in the 1930s. Sociology in the South had a foothold, and it has not looked back. Most of the South's major colleges and universities now have departments (although there are exceptions), and in terms of numbers sociology is thoroughly entrenched.

There was a time, early on, when it looked as if sociology might develop along rather different lines in the South than elsewhere, re-

---

1. The early years of this century saw an organization called the Southern Sociological Congress, but it was a capital-p Progressive movement, staffed largely by Social Gospel clergymen and benevolent laypeople, and was devoted to such worthy causes as the abolition of child labor. It used the word *sociology* to mean roughly what is now designated by *social work*, and it had little to do with what is meant by *sociology* today.

flecting its regional setting, but that did not happen. An article in *The Southern Sociologist* a few years back, based on a national sample of sociologists, showed regional differences within the discipline similar in kind and in magnitude to differences we can find in the general population. The Southerners were more often conventionally religious, more conservative politically, and so forth. But there is no real difference, North and South, in the sort of *sociology* we do. There may be some regional influence on what Southern sociologists choose to study, but the theoretical apparatus and the methodology we bring to that undertaking are the standard, nationally advertised brands—as they should be.

But there remains this matter of a difference in quality. We are doing what sociologists do all over America, but, on the record, we're not doing it *as well*. Why don't Southerners succeed at sociology in the same numbers as we do in, say, history or literature?

Part of the story, to be sure, is simply that sociology is held in lower repute in the South than elsewhere; a classic sociological study of occupational prestige, *Occupations and Social Status*, has shown as much.[2] Obviously there is less inducement for talented young Southerners to take it up. Certainly they wouldn't do it for the money.

But why is this? Why has the South not extended its legendary hospitality to sociology? One reason may be an early confusion with social work, if not with social*ism*, a confusion that persists to this day in the South. (Two-thirds of the sociology majors at my university say they would major in social work if the university would let them, and they sometimes get annoyed when we insist on teaching them things that they see, correctly, as having little to do with their intended careers.) This confusion is so pervasive that it does little good to protest, but I think sociology's reputation suffers because of it. We have enough sins of our own to answer for without being held accountable for what goes on in social-work schools.

There is also this suspicion that sociologists are up to no good politically, and it is a fact that most have left-of-center opinions, views not

---

2. Southerners share this aversion with the English. I once told a clerk at the Bodleian Library that I was reading in the sociology of religion. "Oooo," he said, wrinkling his nose, "that sounds nasty." I soon learned to say that I was doing ecclesiastical history.

welcome in the past in many Southern communities. There is no intrinsic connection between discipline and political stance. In fact, as Robert Nisbet has reminded us in *The Sociological Tradition*, some (maybe most) of the greatest sociologists have been conservatives of one sort or another. And recall that Fitzhugh and Hughes were defending slavery; it's hard to get more conservative than that. But many Southerners in this century have had reason to look at sociology with suspicion, for whatever their politics, sociologists are inclined to examine things that many Southerners would just as soon have left unexamined. So even poor Howard Odum, a very conservative man both by temperament and policy, continually found himself in hot water for imagined offenses (and some of his graduate students' *real* offenses) against the South's racial etiquette, religious orthodoxy, and established patterns of labor relations.

In any case, part of sociology's problem in the South has been one of reputation. But I think there is another reason why the South has never really taken to sociology (and here the *real* speculation begins). I don't think the sociological way of thinking comes as easily to well-acculturated Southerners as to other Americans, just as it doesn't seem to come as easily to Americans in general as it does to Europeans, or to the first- and second-generation Americans who have done most of the creative work in American sociology.

Sociology, like the other social sciences, only perhaps more so, is a *generalizing* discipline. It requires, at least initially, that one ignore the differences between individuals and between groups, and concentrate on what they have in common. At its best, it is supposed to apply abstract theoretical categories to disparate phenomena and to see the underlying similarities among apparently quite different empirical cases. The idiosyncratic features of the things we are observing are supposedly of little interest; indeed, they are a damned nuisance, and our models treat them as "error." Sociology intends to talk about the forest; detailed and loving attention to individual trees is not our business.

Now this isn't a very Southern way to go about things. Southerners are more often brought up, I think, to insist on the sort of detail that social science instructs its practitioners to ignore. In the sociological terms of Talcott Parsons, Southern culture is more "particularistic," less "universalistic," than American culture in general. Whatever your feelings about that, social science (indeed, science of any sort) is universalistic, perhaps to a fault.

Consider a few examples from a variety of contexts of what I mean when I say that Southern culture, black and white, is particularistic. Look first, for example, at country music—still basically the music of the white Southern working class. Compared to American popular music in general, country music lyrics are loaded with details. They less often just express a sentiment; a good deal of the time they are *telling a story*, and in good journalistic style, reporting who, what, when, where, and why. We are not dealing with Everyman, but with particular lovers and fighters and workers. In "Take This Job and Shove It," for instance, Johnny Paycheck isn't complaining about foremen in general, or about a foreman left undescribed so that we can fill in the blanks for ourselves—no, it's *his* foreman, an overbearing SOB with a brand new flattop haircut. This is not a special case of "worker-management conflict," but a particular worker in a particular job. In "Trudy," Charlie Daniels tells us about the villain, Johnny Lee Walker—what kind of car he drives, where he carries his switchblade, what kind of gun he wears under his coat. We're told about his watch chain and his moustache and his tastes in women and whiskey; we hear about his townhouse in Dallas and his hotel suite in New Orleans. We know about the hero, too. Before his encounter with Johnny Lee, we're told, he lost exactly $35 in the slot machine, but turned around and won $110 at seven-card. Eventually the song explains why the hero wound up in jail, and most of us would agree that it's a much more satisfying answer than anything a criminologist could tell us about aggravated assault in a Southwestern Standard Metropolitan Statistical Area.

Southern humor is much the same. It relies very little on one-liners, and if it has any political or ideological content at all, it tends toward anarchy. Mostly, it is a matter of detailed storytelling, with all manner of descriptive excursions. If there's a punch line, it is a long time coming, and it's often pretty lame, but that doesn't matter. When Brother Dave Gardner retells the story of David and Goliath, for instance, the awful pun at the end isn't the point. What is funny are things like his detailed description of the construction of the slingshot out of a blue suede tennis shoe tongue. Brother Dave's account of Julius Caesar's assassination also ends with a sorry pun which isn't the point of the story; we hear him out for things like his description of a Roman bureaucrat's difficulties parking a bicycle. Jerry Clower is a very different sort of humorist, but just as Southern as Brother Dave, and his laughs come from details, too—the morning noises in his neighborhood as housewives pop open cans of biscuits ("sounds like a young war"), or the sound a chain saw makes when it goes through a screen door.

This eye for detail, this concern with telling a story, has a great deal to do, I think, with what black and white Southerners do *well*: journalism and literature, for instance. A while back, in fact, Norman Podhoretz, the editor of *Commentary*, complained that Southerners were taking over the American literary establishment. I think he exaggerated, but there is certainly no question that American journalism owes a great deal to a collection of Southerners that runs the gamut from Hunter Thompson to Tom Wicker to Dan Rather to Tom Wolfe to Jack Kilpatrick. And American letters would be altogether different, and immeasurably poorer, without such figures as William Faulkner, Thomas Wolfe, and Flannery O'Connor, to mention only three of the most accomplished—and deceased. Scholars who are better qualified to say it than I am assure us that there are differences between Southern fiction and other varieties of American fiction. Robert Penn Warren insists, for instance, that Southern literature is marked by a concentration on the idiosyncracies, peculiarities, and downright grotesqueries of individual characters. Southern novelists, it seems, are seldom trying to prove a point or illustrate a thesis; they are trying to tell a story, which is what Southerners like to do, and novelists are supposed to do. Flannery O'Connor said once that people always asked her why Southern authors so often write about freaks; she liked to reply that maybe it's because Southerners can still recognize them. Like the characters in Southern music, the characters in Southern fiction are difficult to mistake for special cases of something-or-other.[3] They are individuals in their own right—often, indeed, extravagantly so. They're interesting precisely because they are *not* typical.

Another place where particularism and an insistence on detail serve

3. Although sometimes non-Southerners make this mistake. I recall the disappointment when I told an audience of English public school boys that the Bundrens, in *As I Lay Dying*, were not a typical Southern family.

Southerners well is in the writing of history, at least in writing history of the old-fashioned sort that is concerned with reporting who did what to whom and when, where, and how. At the fiftieth anniversary celebration of the Southern Historical Collection, C. Vann Woodward spoke of the regional differences among his thirty years' worth of graduate students, many of them now distinguished scholars of Southern history. The Southerners, he said, were likely to be interested in the South per se, telling its story and piling up the facts about it. The non-Southerners were more likely to use the South as a locale for testing hypotheses or arguing a thesis, ignoring or downplaying the details that they found irrelevant but that the Southerners felt were almost the point of the enterprise. Southerners, one gathers, are likely to conclude by summarizing; non-Southerners by generalizing. Compare, for instance, U. B. Phillips' *American Negro Slavery*, a thorough, workmanlike descriptive account of the peculiar institution, to Stanley Elkins' book, called just *Slavery*, with its discussion of the effects of "total institutions" on character and personality, and its controversial analogy between American slavery and the Nazi concentration camps. Both are important works, but in very different ways, and the difference is evident even in their titles. The point is not that the Southerners are "pro-Southern" and non-Southerners "anti-Southern"; Woodward was saying that Southerners tend to approach their subject matter with a different sort of end in view, and his observation is quite consistent with what I am trying to argue about Southern culture generally.

Another enterprise that has attracted more than its share of the South's talent has been the law. You might think that is an exception to the case I am building here, but think again. What is the law concerned with but (in the first instance) establishing what actually happened in a particular case? After that, the question of whether the particular instance falls into a more general category does arise, but at least as much effort is devoted to establishing that it does not—that the particular circumstances make it different—as that it does. To some extent, our laws (and, to a greater extent, our jury decisions) recognize, for instance, that there are murders and, well, there are murders. One should hesitate to generalize. This recognition goes a long way toward explaining why, for forty years, Southerners have been less likely than non-Southerners to tell the Gallup Poll that they approve of capital punishment for murder. It depends.

In *The Enduring South*, I argued that this insistence that apparently similar things are, in fact, not interchangeable has something to do with Southern localism, an attachment to particular places. Two communities may look very similar in instrumental terms—similar kinds and levels of services, similar climates and appearance, similar economies and politics, similar people even—but their connotations are different, they have different histories and different associations in the present. It's a matter not just of what they can do for you, but of what they *are*.

One anthropologist has argued that Southern particularism extends even to objects. Two 1957 Chevrolets may be functionally equivalent in every respect, but one is *mine*, in a sense more fundamental than the name on the title certificate. "The Dukes of Hazzard" television program errs in a lot of details about Southern life, but the relation between Bo and Luke and their car, "General Lee," is the kind of thing I'm talking about. Similarly, although the cult of antiques isn't an exclusively Southern phenomenon, I wonder if in the South it may be less a matter of aesthetics and more one of liking to think about the real or imagined history, the associations and individuality of our old things. You might think that a table is only a table, but tell that to my friend in Columbia whose kitchen table served as a makeshift operating table for a Confederate field hospital.

My point is that I believe Southerners resist the assertion that, if you've seen one slum, one table, one murder, one total institution, one proletarian—one whatever—you've seen them all. This serves us Southerners well in some matters, as I've observed. It is less of an asset in others. For instance, when it comes to taking IQ tests, the skills being measured are precisely those of induction and deduction—generalizing from specific cases to general principles or applying general principles to specific cases—the kind of thing I'm arguing that we tend to resist doing. It should not come as any surprise, then, to observe that Southerners do less well on the average than non-Southerners when this sort of faculty is tested; Southern blacks do less well than non-Southern blacks, and Southern whites do less well than non-Southern whites. IQ tests measure, essentially, the bureaucratic skills: the ability to classify "cases" in terms of general categories, to treat cases in the same category similarly, and not to linger over the details. If the Southern inclination runs more toward the *ad hoc* response, taking all the details into account, custom-tailoring rather than fitting the customer for some off-the-rack category, this may mean, at best, that we are less likely to fold, spindle, and mutilate one another. On the other hand, that sort of thing *is* inefficient, in cost-effectiveness terms, and it can have outcomes that even we Southerners would call favoritism, nepotism, or corruption. Think of Bert Lance and his troubles, for instance, which came about because his relatives were treated specially, individually, rather than as instances of the general category "credit risk."

In Southern politics, this same tendency is evident in the pattern that V. O. Key identified as the "friends and neighbors" vote, in which some area deviates from its traditional voting patterns to support a favorite son. The reasoning seems to be, "Well, he may be one of *them* (another faction in the Democratic party or maybe even a Republican), but we know him—we know his people—he's all right." This sort of exception is practically the rule in Southern politics, although it does have its limits, as Jimmy Carter discovered in 1980.

I'm arguing that we just go in less for categorical thinking, and that includes both theoretical and ideological thought. Certainly, conditions in the South were desperate enough in the 1930s for communism to have made some inroads, but it never really did, despite some serious efforts. Neither did fascism, of the ideologically thoroughgoing variety; that ideology of statism and struggle was as abstract as Communist doctrine, and seemed to most Southerners as irrelevant to their situations. Not that there was not grievance aplenty; rather, it was directed toward particular affronts, particular people, particular practices. When Johnny Paycheck has a complaint about his job, he doesn't ideologize it and join a union or the Communist party; he tells off his foreman and quits. In the old-style Southern industrial enterprise, as W. J. Cash describes it, the bosses were less likely than bosses elsewhere to view their employees as "factors of production" or even as "the workers"; they put up a good front, at least, of regarding them as Jim and Tom and Mary Sue. The workers, in general, returned the favor; it might have been "Mr. Bob," but it wasn't a special case of "the bosses," "the capitalists," or "the oppressors." There has been labor conflict in the South, of course, but it hasn't often been *ideological* conflict; it has been over money, hours, and conditions, and has certainly not been seen as part of a worldwide struggle.

The fact that the South has come out of the civil rights struggle so well, all things considered, may have a lot to do with the fact that things never really got ideological, on either side. Straight conflicts of interest are easier to handle, easier to negotiate, than conflicts in which the parties dehumanize each other with ideology. I think that's what the president of the Afro-American Association at the University of Alabama in the early 1970s was getting at when he said that black and white Southerners are "more basic about their approach to problems." He put it this way: "I find that the brothers in New York and on the West Coast tend to approach their problems from an abstract perspective." Southern blacks see things less ideologically, more particularistically. Northern black activists "go all the way around, so to speak, and then try to hit at the target from the back side or the left side. . . . I just hit it straight on and you can get a direct solution to a problem."

Before I get back to sociology, let me consider one objection (a big one) to this argument. "What do you mean [someone might well ask] that Southerners resist categorical thinking? What could be more categorical than racism? What about the distinction in Southern Protestant theology between the saved and the unsaved? What about the us-against-them mentality that you have said is at the heart of Southern regional identity? It looks to me [this same critic could say] as if Southern culture is nothing *but* a series of oversimplified, dichotomous abstractions."

The accuracy of the observation must be acknowledged. Certainly the official public thought of the South has been dominated by some great and terrible oversimplifications, abstractions imposed like some straitjacket on the concrete particularities of Southern life. But it does seem to me that in general we have not really followed through, that the full inhuman implications of these frightening abstractions have been to some extent mitigated by this very particularism—this seeming illogicality, if you will. We have seen in this century, although not in the South, what happens when racist doctrines are pursued with Germanic thoroughness. We've seen in other times and places what happens when exclusivist religious doctrines are given full sway. We have had only hints in the South of what happens when a people really acts on a conviction that it's them against the world.

It may be that the only way a people as amiable as Southerners can live with doctrines like those that most of us once held (and many still do) is to allow for a great many exceptions and to put our theories into practice as seldom as possible, to try to treat people as Jim and Tom and Mary Sue, rather than as cases of categories we are theoretically bound to despise. All Southern whites know people who believe the most horrible things about black people, for instance, yet still manage to have amicable relations and even genuine friendships with particular blacks. We all know Evangelical Protestants who believe in all sincerity that the unconverted will go to hell, but who don't treat their unconverted friends as hell-bound sinners.

This pattern of not following through goes way back. One of my favorite illustrations has to do with a presentment issued during the Civil War by a grand jury in Talbot County, Georgia, condemning the "evil and unpatriotic conduct of the representatives of Jewish [financial] houses." Lazarus Straus was the patriarch of the only Jewish family in the county and he decided, not surprisingly, to take this sentiment personally. After he announced his intention to move (his son Isidor writes), "Father's action caused such a sensation in the whole county that he was waited on by every member of the grand jury, also by all the ministers of the different denominations, who assured him that nothing was further from the minds of those who drew the presentment than to reflect on father, and that had anyone had the least suspicion that their action could be [so] construed . . . it never would have been permitted to be so worded." (Stephen Whitfield, from whom I heard the story, says you can almost hear the citizens of Talbot County, as the Straus family leaves for New York, to start Macy's department store, saying "Y'all come back.") That's the kind of thing I mean. Even when we deal in generalizations, we're not so rigorous or so adept at applying them. That may be our saving fault.

I realize that I have said more about the South and less about sociology than I intended, but Southern readers are probably more interested in the South than in sociology anyway. Southerners tend to be. That's my point.

But I shall close by getting back to sociology briefly. I'm suggesting that folks who can condemn Jews without realizing that they're likely to offend Lazarus Straus are at a disadvantage in a pursuit that requires them to apply general categories to particular cases. They may be good neighbors. They can be great storytellers, full of surprises. They may even make good lawyers, since they're used to explaining why everything is an exception. But the kind of skill that is rewarded in sociology doesn't come easily to someone who is inclined to think that the most interesting thing about Max Weber is that he had relatives in Mount Airy, North Carolina.

Howard Odum has come up a couple of times in this discussion. He was, in many ways, the founder of modern sociology in the South. But the sociology he wrote himself was odd, by the standards of his discipline. It was a very particularistic sort of thing. Odum wrote about the South, primarily, and he wrote in a form that he practically invented. He called it "portraiture." If you look at *An American Epoch*, *The Way of the South*, *Southern Regions of the United States*, or any of his other works, you shouldn't be surprised to see what this Georgia boy was doing. He was piling on the details, getting it all in, trying to do justice to the complexity of what he was observing. Odum's characteristic device wasn't the statistical table or the chart, but the *list*— hundreds of them, thousands probably. State birds, state flowers, state nicknames, distinguished statesmen, former capitals, principal products—list after list after list, with hardly a generalization and never a hypothesis to be found. The facts, his method seems to assume, will speak for themselves. If they don't, the answer is to collect some more facts. Do I have to point out that this is a very Southern way to do sociology?

But it is not the kind of sociology that gets assistant professors promoted today. And that's a shame, because the kind of work Odum and his students produced had, at its best, narrative power and human interest. It told a story in the best Southern tradition, and it could speak to readers other than sociologists, to people interested in the South as *the South*, for instance, not as a special case of underdevelopment, neocolonialism, a peripheral economy, or whatever. Most of us sociologists today don't have that ability, or have been trained to suppress it. And that's too bad, because whether or not the South needs more sociologists, I suspect sociology needs more Southerners, real ones or spiritual ones—not to take over, not to turn sociology away from universalism, but to divide the labor within our discipline, to tell sociological stories about particular people, particular groups, particular societies. And interesting stories they could be.

II.   Exploring Southern Identity

The Heart of Dixie
An Essay in Folk Geography

In his many writings, Howard Odum often distinguished between "the region determined by technological boundaries or social incidence" (for example, by the horse-to-mule ratio, or by proportion of the labor force in agriculture) and the region as "an extension of the folk." Most sociological attempts to define regions, including Odum's own, have concentrated on definitions of the former sort, which Odum argued was the appropriate basis for social planning, to the neglect of the latter, which he argued was of greater interest to social science. The distinction between the two is not absolute, of course, for if a folk is set apart by distinctive folkways, it may inadvertently reveal itself to the sociologist or geographer who is working with economic, demographic, or technological data. But if Rudolf Heberle was right when he argued some years ago that the sociologically interesting thing about a region is that it may give rise to or contain a regional *group*, then identification and integration with that group would seem to be the sociologically most important criteria for defining a region, and we ought to look at these variables more directly than we have in the past.

The paramount example of a self-conscious regional group in the United States has of course been found in the Southeastern states, and one way to draw the geographical boundaries of the South as "an extension of the folk" would be to define it as "that part of the country where the people think they are Southerners." I tried to employ such a definition in *The Enduring South*, using secondary analysis of existing survey data, but that effort was handicapped from the outset by problems of measurement and sampling. Here I want to suggest an alternative strategy, using a convenient and inexpensive measure of regional identification to address three related questions: 1) where is the South (defined this way)? 2) where is Dixie? and 3) what is the relation between the two?

Table 1. Cities in Sample, Ratio of *Southern* to *American* Entries (*S*), Ratio of *Dixie* to *American* Entries (*D*), and Number of *American* Entries

	S	D	American entries		S	D	American entries
ALABAMA				Durham	76	20	25
Birmingham	86	58	146	Winston-Salem	84	43	37
Montgomery	98	55	49	Fayetteville	93	56	27
Mobile	102	34	58	Greensboro	97	33	64
MISSISSIPPI				*FLORIDA*			
Jackson	86	51	69	St. Petersburg	45	17	75
Biloxi-Gulf Park	96	70	27	West Palm Beach	45	33	87
				Orlando	47	18	139
GEORGIA				Fort Lauderdale	49	11	148
Atlanta	70	22	450	Miami	60	28	257
Columbus	73	49	37	Jacksonville	67	36	132
Savannah	91	50	34	Tampa	69	28	94
Augusta	111	63	36	Pensacola	74	38	39
Macon	116	84	31	Tallahassee	89	26	27
LOUISIANA							
New Orleans	70	33	235	*VIRGINIA*			
Baton Rouge	95	22	46	Roanoke	35	22	55
Shreveport	108	27	66	Norfolk	46	13	111
				Richmond	53	15	130
TENNESSEE							
Nashville	76	28	144	*KENTUCKY*			
Knoxville	81	36	67	Lexington	45	29	56
Memphis	86	42	151	Louisville	46	37	138
Chattanooga	90	48	67	*ARKANSAS*			
SOUTH CAROLINA				Little Rock	53	20	83
Charleston	60	36	50				
Columbia	68	35	77	*TEXAS*			
Greenville	86	39	70	El Paso	4	0	81
				Amarillo	10	0	41
NORTH CAROLINA				Abilene	10	3	39
Asheville	70	14	47	Dallas	19	4	477
Charlotte	72	18	130	San Antonio	21	4	165
Raleigh	74	19	57	Austin	23	3	76

Table 1.   continued

	S	D	American entries		S	D	American entries
Corpus Christi	26	4	65	*MISCELLANEOUS*			
Fort Worth	27	3	122	Duluth, Minn.	0	0	31
Houston	36	13	419	Boise, Idaho	0	0	33
Port Arthur	42	8	24	Grand Rapids, Mich.	0	1	80
Galveston	53	7	30				
				Sioux Falls, S. Dak.	0	4	28
OKLAHOMA				Scranton, Pa.	0	4	69
Oklahoma City	16	1	208	Salt Lake City, Utah	1	0	180
Tulsa	38	6	127				
				Colorado Springs, Colo.	2	0	58
DELAWARE-MARYLAND-D.C.							
Washington	8	1	680	Boston, Mass.	2	0	376
Wilmington	13	0	63	Albuquerque, N. Mex.	2	1	128
Dover	13	2	45				
Baltimore	21	5	346	Buffalo, N.Y.	2	1	156
				St. Paul, Minn.	2	1	170
WEST VIRGINIA-OHIO				Portland, Oreg.	2	1	227
Wheeling	0	0	32	Minneapolis, Minn.	2	1	325
Cleveland	4	1	387				
Columbus	6	3	199	Des Moines, Iowa	2	2	88
Dayton	11	18	105	Omaha, Nebr.	2	2	132
Cincinnati	12	23	212	Spokane, Wash.	3	0	61
Huntington	24	5	21	Newark, N.J.	3	1	182
				San Francisco, Calif.	3	1	416
INDIANA-ILLINOIS							
Peoria	2	2	51	Detroit, Mich.	3	2	475
Chicago	3	0	1153	Las Vegas, Nev.	3	5	59
Indianapolis	11	1	210	Lincoln, Nebr.	4	0	23
Springfield	15	0	46	Philadelphia, Pa.	4	0	502
Evansville	30	2	40	Camden, N.J.	4	1	118
				Pittsburgh, Pa.	5	0	283
MISSOURI-KANSAS				Los Angeles, Calif.	5	2	914
Kansas City (Mo.)	6	3	320				
St. Louis	12	2	379	Rochester, N.Y.	5	4	95
Topeka	13	3	32	Phoenix, Ariz.	6	1	205

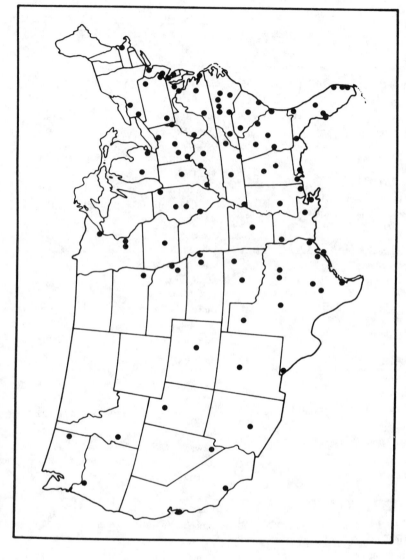

Figure 1.   Location of Data Points

The basic idea is a simple one. Other things equal, residents of Southern areas should be more likely to use the word *Southern* in the names of their businesses, voluntary associations, and so forth, and we can use this fact to fix the points at which people stop thinking of themselves as Southern. We can, obviously, apply the same strategy to the word *Dixie*, and, for reasons I shall offer below, it may be worthwhile to compare the two.

To obtain the data used here, we consulted fairly recent telephone directories from a haphazard, vaguely purposive sample of American cities (see Table 1 and Figure 1).[1] In each, we counted the number of entries beginning with *Southern*, with *Dixie*, and with *American*. We did not count listings in which the word *Southern* modified a state or region (Southern California or Southern New England), strings of entries in which the word was obviously part of the name of a local subdivision (Southern Hills or Southern Acres), or entries for individuals with the last names Southern, Dixie, or American (there were some of each).[2]

Clearly, sheer number of entries is not a good measure of the Southernness of a city (Chicago has more Southern entries than Macon); we need a measure standardized by the total number of nonresidential entries. But since this statistic would have been extraordinarily difficult to obtain for one hundred middling-to-large cities, we compromised, and standarized the number of Southern entries and the number of Dixie entries by dividing each by the number of American entries, on the assumption that the last is roughly proportional to the

1. The directories we used were found in the University of North Carolina, Chapel Hill, library, in the North Carolina State University Alumni Office, and in the course of our travels. We tried to use only large (roughly defined as having more than twenty-five entries beginning with *American*), recent (1971 or later) books, although each criterion was occasionally relaxed to include particularly strategic data points (*e.g.*, six directories were from the middle or late 1960s). We consulted virtually all available directories from the Southeastern and border states (hence, the large number of points in North Carolina), and a geographically scattered sample of directories from elsewhere.
2. Among Cameron Ingram's many contributions to this research was the observation that a disproportionate number of beauticians are named Dixie, a subject itself worthy of further investigation. We intended also to count entries beginning with *Rebel* and *Confederate*, but discovered that such entries are too rare for quantitative purposes.

total number of business entries.[3] The resulting measures, S and D, are displayed in Table 1.

Where Is the South?

Figure 2 is a rough mapping of the value of S, interpolating from the values at the data points shown in Figure 1. By this measure,

Figure 2.   *Southern* Entries as Percentage of *American* Entries

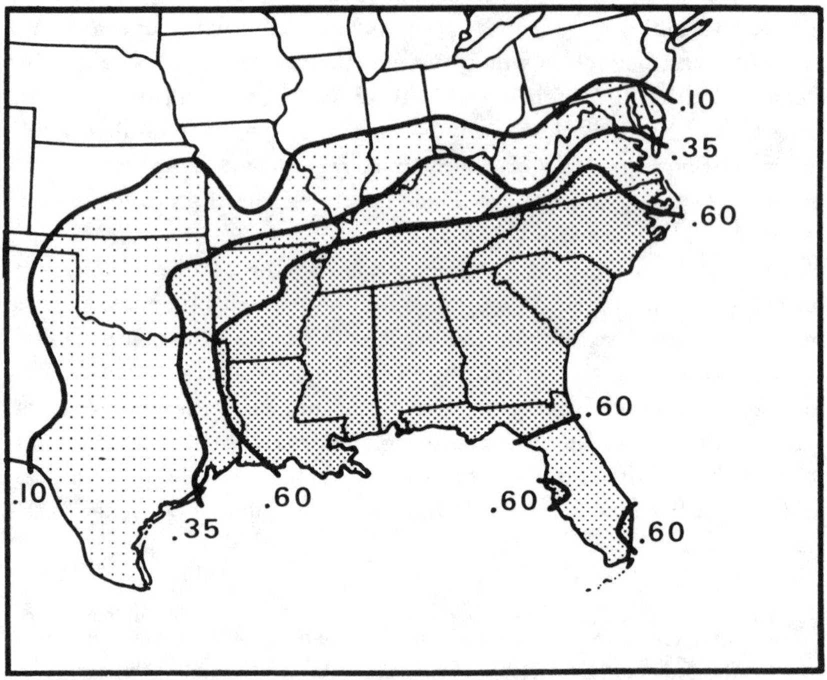

.10
.35
.60
.60
.10
.60
.35
.60
.60

3. Obviously, to the extent that this assumption is incorrect, error is present in our measures, and this may be the reason for the observed differences between, say, Washington and Baltimore, or Dallas and Fort Worth. The measures might more accurately be thought of as tapping regional versus national integration. (See the discussion in the concluding section.) We did attempt an estimate of the total number of entries (commercial and residential), but since the ratio of commercial to residential listings is evidently not at all constant from one directory to another, perhaps it is not surprising that measures standardized by that estimated total did not behave as well as those used here. We did not have access to the yellow pages for many of the cities in our sample, and since these are often for different areas than those covered by the white pages, we probably could not have used them in any case.

at least some degree of Southernness is discernible quite far to the north. However defined, the South is surrounded by a nimbus that takes in Delaware, Maryland, the southern parts of the states from West Virginia to Missouri, and even a fragment of Kansas. To the west, this penumbra is even wider than to the north, and it includes most of Texas and Oklahoma. While we might want to acknowledge that these areas do have some links to the South (and most of them have been tied to the region, historically, by settlement patterns and otherwise), if we are interested in choosing a single contour line as the boundary of *the* South, history—and prudence—dictate a rather less imperialistic definition.

If we inspect the array of S values, there appears to be a modest natural break in the sequence between $S = .30$ (Evansville, Indiana) and $S = .35$ (Roanoke, Virginia), and a contour line at $S = .35$ has some interesting properties. Except in the west, it follows state lines remarkably well, outlining a familiar region: the eleven Southeastern states that Odum identified in the 1930s, in *Southern Regions of the United States*, on the basis of several hundred economic and demographic criteria. All of the data points in these states fall within the line, and none of the points outside these states does, except those in eastern Texas and Oklahoma. While noting some degree of Southernness in and around Houston, Galveston, Port Arthur, and Tulsa, we may have to conclude (as Odum did) that Texas and Oklahoma are, on balance, no longer Southern states. (As it happens, all four of the Texas and Oklahoma cities that fall within the $S = .35$ contour line have more Southern than Western entries in their telephone directories, while only two of the nine cities outside the line do.)

This conclusion is buttressed by the fact that the Southern parts of these states appear to be only marginally Southern, in any case. Further down the array of S values, there is another, and larger, natural break in the sequence: only two cities (Miami and Charleston, South Carolina) have values between .53 and .67. If we draw a contour line at $S = .60$, all of the points in Texas and Oklahoma, the single point in Arkansas (Little Rock), and the points in Kentucky and Virginia fall outside the line; all of the points in Tennessee, North Carolina, and the Deep South states from South Carolina to Louisiana fall inside it; and Florida displays a not-unexpected gradient. (Notice, incidentally, that Florida is at least as Southern, by this measure, as Virginia.) This somewhat more restricted South—not yet Deep, but more than shallow—seems to be defined by the Mississippi River and the 37th parallel, with the rest of Louisiana rather as a lagniappe.

Wading in a little further, those cities with S greater than .85 are nearly all in the conventionally defined Deep South (Table 2), although some surprising cities—among them Charleston, Atlanta, and New Orleans—do not survive that cut. To a very large extent, however, S appears to be inversely correlated with degree of latitude, until the traveler reaches the Florida border.

Perhaps the most interesting thing about Figure 2 is how uninteresting it is. To a great extent, it merely confirms what most students of the South—or tourists, for that matter—already knew, which suggests that S is a reliable and valid measure and that the technique does what it is supposed to do.

The boundaries that it yields for the regional South are remarkably coincident with those that have been drawn by sociologists and geographers who have approached the subject with quite different criteria for Southernness. The Greater South, outlined by the $S = .10$ contour line in Figure 2, approximates what Wilbur Zelinsky identified in his *Cultural Geography of the United States* as the Southern culture area, on the basis of settlement patterns and cultural homogeneity, and, as I have indicated, the contour line for $S = .35$ is virtually identical with the boundary of the Southeast that Howard Odum defined, in effect, as a region with a common set of social problems. In other words, the theoretical possibility that Odum's two sorts of regional definition might give different results does not seem to have been realized in the case

Table 2.   Cities with S Scores Greater Than 0.85

0.86	Greenville, S.C.	0.95	Baton Rouge, La.
0.86	Memphis, Tenn.	0.96	Biloxi-Gulf Park, Miss.
0.86	Jackson, Miss.	0.97	Greensboro, N.C.
0.86	Birmingham, Ala.	0.98	Montgomery, Ala.
0.89	Tallahassee, Fla.	1.02	Mobile, Ala.
0.90	Chattanooga, Tenn.	1.08	Shreveport, La.
0.91	Savannah, Ga.	1.11	Augusta, Ga.
0.93	Fayetteville, N.C.	1.16	Macon, Ga.

of the American South. Regional identity, regional culture, and regional social pathology—all define essentially the same region.

Where Is Dixie?

If we try to use the statistic D to draw a map of Dixie, however, something rather different emerges (Figure 3). Since *Dixie* is almost everywhere a less frequent entry than *Southern* (the average Southern directory has only about 43 percent as many of the former), we should perhaps not make too much, yet, of the fact that D begins to rise above the noise only at points farther east and south than S. Nevertheless, it is true that there is very little use of the word *Dixie* outside the eleven Southeastern states, and, in particular, little in Texas and Oklahoma. Every Southeastern city has a value of D greater than .10, while outside the Southeast only Houston and two Ohio cities on U.S. 25, the Dixie Highway, have values of D that high.[4]

However we define Dixie, its outline is much less regular than that of the South.[5] Its boundaries are less disposed to follow state lines, and there are more ridges and bowls on the contour map. Even the line for $D = .15$ reveals inroads to both the north (Richmond and Norfolk) and south (Fort Lauderdale), while that for $D = .25$ delimits a misshapen doughnut configuration, with Atlanta in the hole, excluding most of Florida, all of Virginia, the one data point in the Appalachian subregion (Asheville, North Carolina), the North Carolina Piedmont (except for an anomaly at Winston-Salem), Little Rock, Louisiana beyond New Orleans, and even Nashville. On the other hand, a ridge extends northward to take in the two Kentucky data points at Lexington and Louisville.

Very high D ratios tend, not surprisingly, to be found in the Deep South (Table 3) and substantially overlap with very high S's, except

4.   These two Ohio cities, Cincinnati and Dayton, were omitted in preparing Figures 3 and 4, since the prevalence of *Dixie* entries in their directories had more to do with the proximity of the highway than with that of Dixie itself. Paul Hemphill has written, in *The Good Old Boys*, about the influence of this highway, and of the migrants who have traveled it, in the life of these cities.

5.   There are no obvious natural breaks in the array of D like those at .35 and .60 for S, so I have allowed the fact that in Southern cities, on the average, D is about 43 percent as great as S to dictate breaks at .15 and .25 (43 percent of .35 and .60, respectively) in Figure 3.

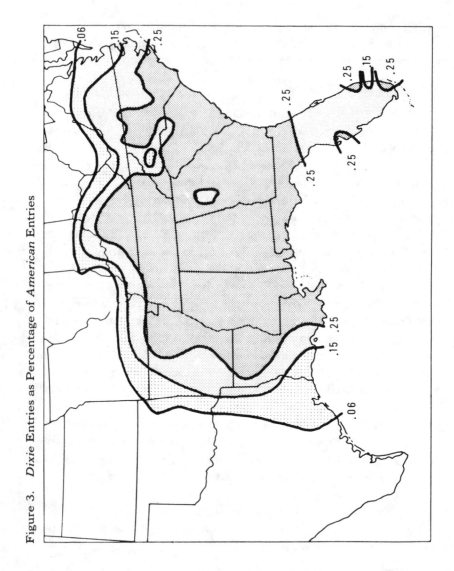

Figure 3.   *Dixie* Entries as Percentage of American Entries

Table 3.   Cities with *D* Scores Greater Than 0.36

0.37	Louisville, Ky.	0.50	Savannah, Ga.
0.38	Pensacola, Fla.	0.51	Jackson, Miss.
0.39	Greenville, S.C.	0.55	Montgomery, Ala.
0.42	Memphis, Tenn.	0.56	Fayetteville, N.C.
0.43	Winston-Salem, N.C.	0.58	Birmingham, Ala.
0.48	Chattanooga, Tenn.	0.63	Augusta, Ga.
0.49	Columbus, Ga.	0.70	Biloxi-Gulf Park, Miss.
		0.84	Macon, Ga.

that none of the Louisiana cities qualifies (not even New Orleans, where, according to one theory, the word *Dixie* was coined), and Louisville, Kentucky, does. Alabama's claim on its license plates to be "the heart of Dixie" appears to be legitimate.

The South Versus Dixie

The fact that Dixie and the South are not altogether coterminous suggests an interesting line of speculation and requires that we consider further what it means when an entrepreneur names his business "Southern XYZ, Inc.," or the "Dixie ABC Company," and what it means when a city has a great many of one or the other or both.

How does an organization come to be tagged Southern? Presumably, such names come about in two different ways. Some designate organizations that are, or aspire to be, regional in scope (Southern Bell, Southern Christian Leadership Conference, Southern Association of Agricultural Scientists); others, apparently, are named in a burst of regional patriotism (Southern Breezes Motel, Southern Fruit and News, Southern Comfort Massage Parlor). The prevalence of the former indicates the extent of a city's integration into the region's economic and social structure; the latter can serve to indicate local businessmen's identification with the regional group—or, perhaps, their perception of such identification among their potential customers. This modest measure, in other words, bears the heavy theoretical weight of indicating both instrumental and affective ties to the region (or, if you prefer, both organic and mechanical solidarity).

Dixie, on the other hand, seems to me to be a purer measure. A business or organization may use *Southern* in its name simply as a descriptive term, but *Dixie* is less likely to be used that way. The dual nature of the word *Southern* and the less ambiguous connotations of *Dixie* mean that while *Southern* can usually be substituted for *Dixie*, the converse is not always true. For example, try substituting *Dixie* for *Southern* in the (genuine) organization names in the preceding paragraph. *Dixie*, in the name of an organization, links it to a symbol of the region's historic culture, a linkage that is often irrelevant and sometimes downright inappropriate. *Dixie* is, as one journalist observed, "a *meaner* word" than *Southern*.

If this line of reasoning is correct, it makes sense that *Southern* entries should be in large measure a matter of geographic location, of proximity to the region's commercial centers and major markets, but *Dixie*, one might say, has more to do with attitude than latitude. To borrow Odum's famous, if cloudy, distinction between regionalism and sectionalism, S measures a mixture of both, while D is more unambiguously a measure of the latter. In general, the two measures are highly correlated—areas central to the Southern economy appear also to be more highly identified with the regional culture—and, indeed, we have it on good authority that where your treasure is, there will your heart be also. But a comparison of Figures 2 and 3 suggests that the correspondence is only approximate; some areas are not as highly identified with the old regional culture as their economic linkage to the region might lead us to suppose, while others have their hearts in Dixie but their assets somewhere else. We may be able to use the relative values of S and D to locate areas of each type.

Table 4 shows that the positive relation between the two measures is, by and large, positively accelerated. Areas on the fringe of the South (S between .10 and .34) should be linked to the South almost exclusively by economic and organizational ties; and in the directories of the seventeen cities of the fringe (leaving out the two on the Dixie Highway), there are only two *Dixie* entries for every eleven beginning with *Southern*—a ratio even lower than that prevailing in the 35 cities outside the Southern sphere of influence altogether (S less than .10), where occasional branch offices or homesick migrants produce "noise" at the ratio of two *Dixies* for seven *Southerns*. As we move into the South proper, D increases to about 40 percent of the value of S, and

Table 4. Relation of *Dixie* to *Southern* Entries, by *S*

S	0–9	10–34	35–59	60–84	85+
Number of cities	35	17*	14	16	16
Total Dixie entries	88	75	279	525	446
Total Southern entries	314	416	709	1294	901
Ratio	.28	.18	.39	.41	.50

* Cincinnati and Dayton excluded.

stays about the same, relatively, until we reach the Deep South (*S* greater than .85), where we find one *Dixie* for every two *Southerns*.

Figure 4 illustrates the general pattern within the South and highlights some interesting exceptions. It shows that high values of *D*, relative to *S*, can be found where both *S* and *D* are highest—in the subregion stretching from eastern North Carolina along the Atlantic seaboard and then west through the Black Belt of the Deep South to the Mississippi (but no further), an area roughly coterminous with the eastern portion of the Cotton South, historically the area of plantation agriculture and largely black population. Relatively high values of *D* are also found in Kentucky—only marginally Southern, but comfortably part of Dixie—and along the course of the Dixie Highway through Ohio.

Markedly low values of *D*, relative to *S*, are found in Evansville, Indiana (the southernmost of the non-Southern cities to the north), in isolated cities in Florida and on the Gulf Coast, and—perhaps not surprisingly—in the one Appalachian city in the sample (Asheville, North Carolina). In addition, lower than expected values of *D* are found in east Texas and Oklahoma, and in Virginia east of the Blue Ridge, areas about as Southern as Kentucky, but less allied to Dixie. Relatively low values of *D* extend from both of these subregions into the Southern heartland, to Shreveport and Baton Rouge, and into the industrial Piedmont of North Carolina. Atlanta, as might be expected from its influence both in the Southern economy and in the recent social history of the region, is represented as an isolated bowl in the—elevated—Deep South. To borrow a distinction from small-group psychology, Atlanta is probably the task leader of the South (its directory has 315

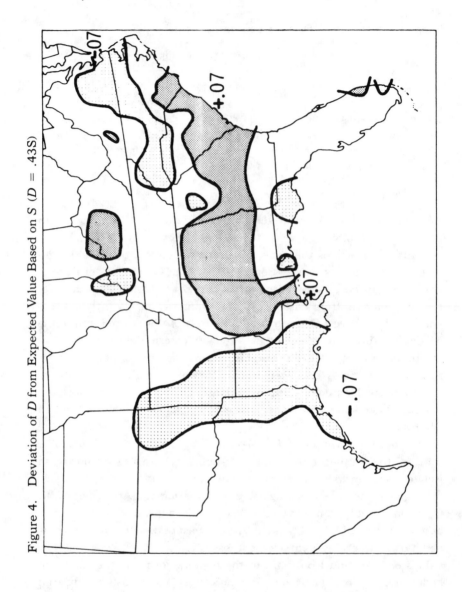

Figure 4.   Deviation of *D* from Expected Value Based on *S* (*D* = .43S)

Southern entries—nearly twice as many as New Orleans, its closest rival), but it is less clearly the socioemotional leader of the region (Birmingham has almost as many *Dixie* listings).

All of this rests, of course, on a somewhat labored interpretation of what it is that *D* and *S* are measuring. Nevertheless, Figure 4 does make a great deal of sense. We can almost label areas with relatively high *S* values the New South, and those with high *D* values the Old South. On the one hand, we find the industrial crescent from Richmond to Atlanta, and the booming Southwest; on the other, the plantation South extending from the coastal plain of North Carolina to the Mississippi, with Kentucky tagging along in remorse for not having joined the Confederacy.[6]

A word about Florida: while the overall pattern for Florida makes sense, there are more anomalies there than anywhere else. I leave it to someone more acquainted with the state's local lore to explain why West Palm Beach should embrace *Dixie* while Fort Lauderdale shuns it, or why Tampa should be more Southern than Saint Petersburg, but I want to suggest that in peninsular Florida, an area of late settlement and heavy immigration, sheer location may have less to do with the character of cities than it does elsewhere in the South. To the extent— and it appears to be considerable—that the South extends into Florida, it may do so as what Zelinsky has called a "voluntary region."

Conclusion

I hope that this speculative attempt to explain the discrepancies between the map of the South and that of Dixie has not distracted the reader from what I regard as this essay's more important contributions: mapping the South as a social-psychological entity, and introducing and validating a technique suitable, I think, for much wider application.

Several problems of the technique still need to be worked out. In

---

6. This observation suggests we may simply be observing a measure of commercial activity. If the word *Dixie* is going out of style, cities with many new enterprises will show smaller ratios of *Dixie* to both *American* and *Southern* than will cities where more businesses were named some time ago. It would be worthwhile and straightforward to see whether, in fact, such a change is taking place. If it is, it could very well be happening faster in some parts of the South than in others.

particular, the assumption that *American* entries are proportional to total nonresidential listings, while apparently good enough for present purposes, is obviously crude—and in fact that ratio, American to total, could itself be mapped as an index of integration into the *national* system. Also, the restriction of attention to cities with fairly large directories is irksome; in this case, it precluded satisfactory attention to the Appalachian subregion. The obvious solution is to pool the entries from smaller cities (as, in fact, we did in the case of Biloxi and Gulf Park, Mississippi), but it is quite possible that size of place has as much to do with integration into a region as does location. By looking only at largish cities, we have in effect controlled for size, but at the risk of implying things that may not be true about small towns and rural areas. Pooling might also obscure some interesting local differences. In this investigation we purposely did not pool, in order to be able to show that Minneapolis looks like Saint Paul, and Durham like Raleigh— good checks on the reliability of our measures. But Tampa did not look like Saint Petersburg, a fact that I am told makes sense, and one we would have overlooked had we ignorantly thrown the two together as a west central Florida point.

Still, the results of this modest inquiry suggest that *S, D,* and other, analogous indices can be valid and sensitive measures. This technique could be extended easily and profitably to the study of other regions, using both drab, functional terms like *Southeastern* and *Pacific* and meatier, folk terms like *Yankee* or *Frontier*. New England should not be very interesting, but I, for one, have never been sure exactly where the Midwest is. Mapping aside, if these measures can be taken to indicate local attachment, they might be used to study quantitatively the state loyalties that bemused Odum in the 1930s. Words like *Hoosier, Tar Heel, Lone Star,* and the like could be used to study variation both among and within states. Moreover, there is the sort of historical inquiry suggested by the fact that in the late 1960s Dallas had somewhat more *Southern* than *Western* entries in its telephone directory, but by 1974 had a shade more of the latter. While it is probably not legitimate to say that the boundary between South and West used to run between Dallas and Fort Worth, but has now moved east, *something* is happening to Dallas, and the South may be shrinking. This technique could be used to illuminate those problems, and many like them.

Harold Isaacs, a political scientist who has written extensively on group identity, put the case for this sort of investigation well, if unintentionally, in his book *Idols of the Tribe*. "Names keep turning up in one way or another in all the ongoing rediscoveries, revisions, remakings, and reassertions of group identities. The name of a country, of an individual, of a group, carries in it all the cargo of the past. A name will seldom itself be the heart of the matter of group identity, but it can often take us to where the heart can be found, leading us deep into the history, the relationships, and the emotions that lie at the center of any such affair."

5.   The Cardinal Test of a Southerner?

Sociologists who have studied the American South have, by and large, been inclined to attribute cultural differences between white Southerners and other Americans to regional differences in occupational structure and economic circumstance. With the economic development and "national incorporation" of the South proceeding apace, advocates of this view assume that regional cultural differences are also diminishing. Indeed, many of the most dramatic and visible ones have been, but an accumulating body of literature demonstrates that many, more subtle, regional cultural differences not only remain but show no sign of disappearing. This suggests that the orthodox materialist view is, at the very least, inadequate and that we must look elsewhere for the explanation of some white Southern peculiarities.

White Southerners are not the only group in America that has surprised sociologists by maintaining its identity and distinctiveness. Since the 1960s, especially, we have come to realize that many immigrant ethnic groups are still intact, and that these groups still serve their members both as social contexts and as psychological entities around which sentiments are organized. Add to these observations the fact that many black Americans have come to believe that the group identity and cohesiveness forced upon them in the past may actually serve, with some modifications, as a valuable resource in the future, and it is not surprising that American sociology has begun to take seriously again the concept of ethnicity.

With these developments in sociology, it was perhaps inevitable that a few would begin to heed the argument of certain historians and journalists that white Southerners can be regarded as an ethnic group, serving the same functions for its members and related to the American majority in much the same way as groups more conventionally considered ethnic, such as Irish-, Polish-, and Lithuanian-Americans.

Analogies can be misleading, of course, but there is already considerable evidence that this is a valuable one. Lewis Killian has used it most persuasively to discuss the situation of white Southern migrants to large Northern cities, and it helps make sense of the large and persistent cultural differences between white Southerners and other Americans—not so much by explaining them as by placing them in a more general category of puzzling phenomena.

Perhaps the most critical questions for the ethnic analogy concern the extent and nature of identification with the group. Milton Gordon has observed, in *Assimilation in American Life*, that the defining characteristic of an ethnic group is that "through historical circumstances, a sense of peoplehood [characterizes its members], a special sense of both ancestral and future-oriented identification with the group." The South has surely had the historical circumstances, but to what extent do Southerners feel a sense of peoplehood—and to what extent does that sense stem from their group's history, independent of current sectional conflict?

The Index of Group Identification

We are fortunate in having at hand a measure of group identification that, although it may lack precision, has the advantage of having been used on several different populations. Angus Campbell and his colleagues, authors of *The American Voter*, report that they measured group identification by asking members of various politically significant groups the following questions: 1) "Would you say that you feel pretty close to [e.g.] Negroes in general or that you don't feel much closer to them than you do to other kinds of people?" and 2) "How much interest would you say you have in how [e.g.] Negroes as a whole are getting along in this country? Do you have a good deal of interest in it, some interest, or not much interest at all?"

Responses to these two questions were used to construct an index that, on the face of it, seems to convey nearly all of what we have in mind when we speak of a person's "attachment" (whether affective or instrumental) to his group. The index was used imaginatively in *The American Voter*, with results that provide further evidence for its validity.

In 1961, Donald Matthews and James Prothro, in the course of an inquiry that led to their book, *Negroes and the New Southern Politics*, asked the same two questions of a sample of 694 white residents of the eleven ex-Confederate states. (The referent, by the way, was Southerners—not white Southerners specifically.) I obtained their data for secondary analysis from the Louis Harris Political Data Center at the University of North Carolina, Chapel Hill.

The data reveal, first, that group identification in this sample of white Southerners is quite high, by this measure. The average group identification score of the 681 respondents who answered both questions is higher than that reported for Catholics and union members in *The American Voter*, and it approaches the scores of Jews and non-Southern blacks. (In terms of response patterns, 41 percent of the respondents indicated the highest possible level of identification—saying they "feel closer to [Southerners than] to other people" and have "a good deal of interest" in how "Southerners as a whole are getting along in this country"; and 56 percent said they feel close to other Southerners and have at least "some interest" in how Southerners are getting along.[1]

Two obvious correlates of this index can serve to suggest that it is valid. In the first place, it is related to birthplace. An analysis reported in *The Enduring South* shows that migrants to the South score markedly lower than natives, as might be expected. Another indication of the index's validity comes from the data in Table 5. As might have been predicted, those who report the highest level of identification are twice as likely as those who report the lowest level to say that the public problems they talk about with their friends are Southern problems.[2] Note, however, that they are no less—and perhaps more—likely

---

1. Nearly all of the respondents fell into one of these categories (scored as indicated):

Score	4	3	2	1	0
Feel Closer	yes	yes	no	no	no
Interest	great	some	great	some	little

This scoring procedure is slightly different from that used by Angus Campbell *et al.*, in *The American Voter*, which did not distinguish between those patterns scored 1 and 2 above. Also, in this analysis, I have used the median as a measure of central tendency.

2. There is little indication from the codebook which responses fell in this category. It does include, however, responses of "segregation," unless the reference was to the local situation. ("Segregation in schools" was considered a local problem.)
    Other response categories, which showed little difference between high and low

Table 5.   Southern Identity and the Level of Public Problems
Discussed

| Southern Identity | Level of Public Problems Discussed[a] | | | | |
	Local	Southern	National	International	(N)[b]
High Scorers (Score of 4 on 4-Point Scale)	13%	12	19	36	(242)
Medium Scorers (Scores of 1–3 on 4-Point Scale)	17%	8	18	37	(282)
Low Scorers (Score of 0 on 4-Point Scale)	24%	6	18	29	(49)

[a]Measured by the question: "When you talk with your friends, do you ever talk about public problems, that is, what's happening in the country or in this community? What public problems do you talk about?" Highest level of first problem mentioned, for high and low identifiers. Responses of "Don't know" and "Don't talk about problems" were excluded from the tables.

[b]N corresponds to 100 percent for each row. Percentages do not add to 100, since categories for which there was no difference between high and low scorers are omitted.

to talk with their friends about international problems. The difference is made up in discussion of strictly local problems; those who exhibit low regional identity are more likely than those with high regional identity to discuss problems of their local community. The differences are not large, and should not be overinterpreted. However, they do suggest that for many Southerners the alternative to thinking in regional terms is not "cosmopolitanism" but even greater "localism."

If the validity of this measure is accepted as demonstrated—it is quite responsive to where one was raised and related to one's focus of attention—we can turn to an examination of correlates that may be a little less obvious.

scores, are "personal and family," "neighborhood," "state," and a residual class for other, unclassified responses (e.g., "taxes").

Correlates of Southern Identification

Here there are some surprises. Matthews and Prothro demonstrated that, as late as 1963, Democrats scored higher on this index than Republicans or Independents; and later analysis showed that Protestants (especially Baptists) scored higher than non-Protestants. But these associations need to be controlled for region of origin and are almost inevitable, given the dominance of Democrats and Protestants in the region. (Ninety percent of the sample were Protestant—40 percent Baptist—and 61 percent were Democrats.) With these exceptions and one other, however, the index of group identification is not strongly related to any of the available background data. Occupation, income, education, urban or rural residence, age, sex—none makes any appreciable difference in scores on the index.

It may be, as suggested above, that the absence of this identification takes different forms in different strata of Southern society (the urban businessman who rejects identification as a Southerner may be nationalist or internationalist, while the small farmer who rejects the label may think of himself instead as primarily a citizen of his county), but Southern identification is present to about the same extent throughout the population. In other words, a relatively high level of group identification exists among white Southerners and cuts across all divisions of society. Whatever grounds for polarization exist in the South, this is evidently not one of them—or, at any rate, was not in 1963.

The only strong correlate of Southern identification in these data, other than the two noted above, is geographic residence within the South. The areas of low Southern identification are where one might expect them to be: Appalachia, southern Florida, and western Texas. A belt of high Southern identification follows the area of cotton cultivation and dense black population—an arc from eastern North Carolina through the Deep South into eastern Texas, with extensions north and south along the Mississippi.

The Cardinal Test

Assuming that Southern identification is not simply translatable as localism, we find no readily available theory to predict what its social correlates might be, and it seems to have few in any event.

There is more reason to expect that it is associated with certain social-psychological measures—support for white supremacy and opposition to racial desegregation, in particular.

There are several lines of thought that might lead to this prediction. In a well-known essay, "The Central Theme of Southern History," the distinguished Southern historian, U. B. Phillips, argued in 1928 that the unity of the white South rested above all else on "a common resolve indomitably maintained—that it shall be and remain a white man's country. . . . The consciousness of a function in these premises, whether expressed with the frenzy of a demagogue or maintained with a patrician's quietude, is the cardinal test of a Southerner." Certainly, many before and since Phillips have suggested that "correct" racial views are the essence of white Southern identity. As stated in sociological terms by the authors of *The American Voter*, "The higher the identification of the individual with his group, the higher the probability that he will think and behave in ways which distinguish members of his group from nonmembers." (In 1963, support for segregation certainly distinguished Southerners from non-Southerners. When asked "Are you in favor of strict segregation, integration, or something in between?" 67 percent of this sample answered "Strict segregation." Using a somewhat more inclusive definition of the South, Herbert H. Hyman and Paul B. Sheatsley reported in *Scientific American* that, in the same year, 68 percent of white Southerners replied "Separate" or "Don't know" when asked "Do you think white and Negro students should go to the same schools or to separate schools?"

There is a supplementary line of reasoning, which could be based on any of several cognitive consistency theories, for expecting that racial views might have something to do with one's feelings toward fellow white Southerners. If one's perception is that blacks and Southern whites have frequently been antagonists, positive feelings toward one group should, according to these theories, tend to produce negative feelings toward the other group. This makes a plausible hypothesis of Gunnar Myrdal's belief, expressed in *An American Dilemma*, that "in general, a friendly attitude toward the South carried with it unfavorable views toward Negroes."

Finally, the geographic distribution of high Southern identification—concentrated in the Southern Black Belt—supports the notion that segregationist views and Southern identification should be positively associated. Table 6 shows that these variables are, in fact, associated. Segregationists score an average of 3.3 on the 4-point scale; those who support something "in between" segregation and integration, and the few outright integrationists in the sample, have median scores of 2.4 and 2.1, respectively. (The association is not terribly strong, however, and certainly not as strong as Phillips' assertion suggests. Gamma, a measure of association that ranges from 0 to 1, is a moderate 0.23.)

We must turn next to the question of whether this association reflects, as Phillips and others imply, a causal connection between the two variables. Is attitude toward race truly the cardinal test it is alleged to be? The question is far from academic. The ethnic group model postulates that the feeling of group identification is based on something other than current, and possibly transitory, common interests; that the group's history contributes to the sense of "we-ness" other than by putting most group members in the same contemporary boat. Also, if Southern identification is dependent on support for racial segregation, the identification will vanish if the support does (and Southern support for segregation is clearly on the wane). On the other hand, if the association is spurious, if it comes about because some other factor leads to both regional identification and support for segregation, the decline of traditional Southern racial practices will not necessarily spell the end of the white South as a self-conscious sectional group.

When we control the two-variable table for region of origin, in Table 7, the association between the two variables disappears entirely for those raised outside the South, and is substantially reduced for native Southerners. In other words, much of the original association came

Table 6.   Southern Identity, by Attitude Toward Segregation

Attitude Toward Segregation	Percent Scoring 4 (Maximum) on Identity Index	Median Score on Identity Index	(N)
Support strict segregation	47%	3.3	(436)
Support "something in between"	34%	2.4	(191)
Support integration	23%	2.1	(44)
Gamma = 0.23			

about because persons raised outside the South are less likely to support segregation *and* less likely to evince Southern identification.

Even the slight association that remains for native Southerners turns out to be spurious. Table 8, controlling for context within the South, reveals that this association is due entirely to the fact that areas within the South that contain large numbers of segregationists are also areas that contain large numbers of people who identify themselves with the South.[3] Within any given community, there is little or no relation between the racial views of individuals and their identification.

Summary and Implications

It appears that the sociological apparatus built around the idea of ethnicity can be applied profitably to the study of white Southern-

Table 7. Southern Identity, by Attitude Toward Segregation, Controlling for Region Where Respondent Was Raised

Attitude Toward Segregation	Percent Scoring 4 (Maximum) on Identity Index		Median Score on Identity Index		(N)	
	Raised in South	Non-South	Raised in South	Non-South	Raised in South	Non-South
Support strict segregation	50%	27%	3.5	1.8	(388)	(48)
Support "something in between"	45%	10%	3.2	1.3	(130)	(61)
Support integration	30%	17%	2.3	2.0	(20)	(24)
Gamma: for Southern-raised = 0.11						
for non-Southern-raised = 0.02						

3. The self-report of context appears to be quite accurate. If primary sampling units are ranked by the proportion of respondents within each who support segregation, the 256 respondents from the most segregationist PSUs (85 percent of whom support segregation) are quite likely to perceive great support for segregation in their communities (56 percent say "all" or "nearly all" support segregation, and 93 percent say that at least "most" support it). Of the 263 respondents from the less segregationist areas (60 percent of whom support segregation), only 21 percent say "all" white people around them are segregationists (58 percent say "most" are, 21 percent say "about half" or "less than half" are).

Table 8.   Southern Identity, by Attitude Toward Segregation,
Controlling for Context,[a] for Respondents Raised in the
South

	Percent Scoring 4 on Identity Index		Median Score on Identity Index		(N)	
	Context		Context		Context	
	Segre-gationist	Mixed	Segre-gationist	Mixed	Segre-gationist	Mixed
Support strict segregation	52%	25%	3.6	2.2	(355)	(24)
Support "something in betweeen"	47%	40%	3.3	2.4	(87)	(35)
Support integration	——[b]	29%	——[b]	2.0	(6)	(14)

Gamma: for respondents from segregationist contexts = 0.060
        for respondents from mixed contexts = −0.004

[a]Measured by the question: "In general, how many of the white people in this area would you say are in favor of strict segregation of the races—all of them, most of them, about half, or less than half of them?" Responses of "all" and "most" constitute a segregationist context, other responses a mixed context. Responses of "don't know" were excluded from the table.

[b]N too small for computation of a stable figure.

ers. The group, we have seen, is characterized by a surprisingly high level of identification by its members, crosscutting (as an ethnic group identification should) class, sex, and age lines. Although this identification undoubtedly responds to the currents of American sectionalism, it is not dependent on one's holding a "correct" ideological position. Its roots must be sought elsewhere. The ethnic analogy suggests that we turn to the group's history and to the socialization processes that lead both Southerners and non-Southerners to think of Southerners as "different."

If the sociological concept of ethnicity can contribute to the study of white Southerners, the study of white Southerners may also contribute to the body of theory on ethnicity. Legal scholars tell us that hard cases make poor law, but this may not be true in social science. The usefulness of a general concept like ethnic group may be most clearly tested when it is used to study a group at the outer margins of its applicability. If the concept is fruitful there, its generality and utility may be assumed.

6. Getting To Know You
Regional Stereotyping Among Southern Whites

In 1970, a sample of white Southern college students was given the inventory of traits used in a classic study of ethnic stereotypes in the 1930s by Daniel Katz and Kenneth Braley. These students were asked to indicate the "typical traits" of the same groups evaluated in the earlier study and, in addition, those of white Southerners and white Northerners. The results, reported in *The Enduring South*, were not unexpected. Southerners were seen as conservative, tradition-loving, courteous, loyal to family ties, conventional, generous, lazy, faithful, very religious, ignorant, stubborn, extremely nationalistic, jovial, and honest (the adjectives are those of Katz and Braley); Northerners as industrious, sophisticated, aggressive, progressive, conceited, ostentatious, argumentive, rude, materialistic, loud, ambitious, arrogant, deceitful, and mercenary. These regional stereotypes were relatively well defined and widely shared (these subjects showed more agreement on typical Northern and Southern traits than on typical black traits), and the characterizations offer few surprises to the student of American sectional relations, since they have been around in much their present form since the antebellum period.

A 1971 sample survey of adult North Carolinians, known as the Survey of North Carolina, offered the opportunity to examine some of the antecedents of regional stereotyping.[1] In particular, we wanted to see

1. The survey was conducted by the Institute for Research in Social Science of the University of North Carolina, Chapel Hill, and was directed by Angell Beza. Interviews were conducted with an area probability sample of the state's adult, noninstitutionalized population. The data reported here come from the 82 percent of white respondents who replied affirmatively to the following: "Some people around here think of themselves as Southerners, others do not. How about you—would you say that you are a Southerner or not?" Responses to this question show a strong (though not perfect) relation to residential history, and it is arguably the best single measure for locating Southerners in inquiries of this sort.

whether exposure to non-Southerners and interaction with them led to a decrease in the likelihood that Southerners would describe them in stereotypical terms, as some versions of the so-called contact hypothesis would predict.

The Contact Hypothesis

The idea that sheer interaction between members of different racial and ethnic groups might reduce prejudice is appealing, not least for its simplicity. Reviews of the literature on the contact hypothesis show that research along these lines was being done as early as the 1930s, although the bulk of articles on the topic appeared in the decade after the 1949 report by Robert Merton and his colleagues on their Hilltown study. From time to time, research on the subject is still reported—as it should be, since there are still unresolved questions about the conditions under which the hypothesis operates as stipulated.

It appears, however, that it often does work. A typical finding is that reported by Robin Williams in *Strangers Next Door*, after examining attitudes toward blacks, Jews, and Mexican-Americans in four communities. "Out of hundreds of tabulations, there emerges the major finding that *in all the surveys in all communities and for all groups, majority and minorities, the greater the frequency of interaction, the lower the prevalence of ethnic prejudice*." The mechanisms that underlie that frequent finding, however, have more often been assumed than studied directly.

One common, and common-sensical, explanation has it that equal-status, cooperative interaction breaks down preexisting derogatory stereotypes, producing in turn positive changes in attitude. Although this assumes that stereotypes are 1) preexisting, 2) derogatory, and 3) inaccurate, those assumptions are probably correct in most of the cases studied by contact hypothesis researchers, who have generally dealt with the attitudes of whites in black-white interaction, or with those of gentiles in Jewish-gentile interaction.

This explanation also assumes that changes in beliefs about some group (cognition) will produce changes in attitudes toward that group (affect, or evaluation). Although it is a social-psychological commonplace that cognition and affect are often empirically as well as analytically independent, it seems reasonable to suppose that if someone has an inaccurate and invidious idea about what members of some group are like, interacting with them as equals on some joint task might well change his beliefs about them, and changed beliefs might produce more favorable attitudes toward the whole group. (Of course, there could be other outcomes. Williams discusses exemption mechanisms—the "some of my best friends are" pattern, for instance. Another possibility is the differentiation of one stereotype into two or more, for example, one for middle-class blacks and another for lower-class ones.) In any case, the usual finding of research on the contact hypothesis is that interaction is associated with more favorable attitudes and less derogatory stereotypes (as judged, usually, by the researcher), although, as Williams notes, the causal direction is not always unambiguously from interaction to change in stereotype to more favorable attitude.

Although research on black-white or Jewish-gentile interaction may be of great practical importance, however, examining only situations like these effectively "controls away" a number of interesting factors. What happens, for instance, when the parties to an interaction have no preexisting stereotype of each other's groups? Might we find that contact produces a stereotype where none existed before? If so, what happens to the affective component of the individual's attitudes?

Sociologists should be the first to acknowledge that there are often real differences, on the average, between racial and ethnic groups, and one way for someone to learn about these differences is to interact with members of another group and to generalize from that experience. If we can find a situation in which the members of one group do not have *any* particular cognitive representation of another group, and if the two groups actually do differ from one another, we might well expect that interaction would, at least at first, give rise to generalizations about the other group—generalizations that very well might resemble the conventional stereotype embedded in folklore or portrayed by the communications media. This is not to revive the "kernel of truth" theory of stereotyping, but merely to observe that when there is a kernel, or a bushel, of truth, we ignore it at peril to our predictions.

One of the very few researchers who has dealt seriously with this problem is Harry Triandis, who has offered the useful distinction between group stereotypes that are "normative"—that is, prescribed as the "appropriate" way to think of group differences—and those that are more or less left up to individuals. Normative stereotypes, we may suppose, are reflected in a group's folklore and in its mass media; nonnormative stereotypes are developed more idiosyncratically by individuals from their own varied experience. The importance of this distinction stems from Triandis' assertion that normative stereotypes will tend to overstate the actual differences between two groups. In situations where a stereotype is culturally prescribed, the effect of interaction will be to undermine it. On the other hand, where there is no culturally prescribed stereotype, the effects of interaction between two groups that actually differ from one another will be to accentuate the stereotype. Triandis argues that Greeks' stereotype of Americans is normative, but that Americans' stereotype of Greeks is not, and demonstrates that the effects of interaction are as his theory would predict. His finding that Americans' stereotyping of Greeks increases with exposure to them is one of the few cases where this result of interaction has been reported.

Application to Sectional Stereotypes

I have argued that many general questions about ethnic group relations can be studied profitably in the context of American sectional relations, and this is a case in point. Although American regional groups are at the outer bounds of the applicability of the ethnic group concept, some of the difficulties involved in studying, say, black-white relations do not arise in studying relations between Southerners and non-Southerners. In particular, there seem to be few social pressures operating to inhibit or to encourage the expression of sectional hostility and derogatory views of other sectional groups, and there is considerable variation within the population in the amount of interregional contact and exposure. In addition, recent evidence indicates that cultural differences between white Southerners and other white Americans are large, as group differences go in the United States.

Moreover, it appears that Southerners' stereotypes of Northerners may be, in Triandis' terms, nonnormative. A 1957 Gallup Poll analyzed in *The Enduring South* showed that more than 20 percent of white Southern respondents were unable to answer when asked "What do you think of Northerners generally?" and another 12 percent asserted that there were no regional differences worth mentioning.

Somewhat smaller proportions of non-Southerners gave these answers when asked about Southerners. In an unpublished study of the sectional stereotypes held by Northern and Southern college students, Gail Wood found that Northern students took their impressions of Southerners from literature and the mass media (especially movies), while Southern students reported that their principal source of information about regional differences was personal contact, which suggests that Northerners' stereotypes of Southerners are normative, but Southerners' stereotypes of Northerners are not.[2] As Triandis' theory would predict (although Wood did not cast it in those terms), the effect of exposure to Southerners was to weaken the stereotypes held by non-Southerners, while the initial effect of exposure to non-Southerners was to *increase* the likelihood that Southerners would trade in conventional generalizations about regional differences. At the extreme high end of the exposure continuum, however, Wood found that contact decreased stereotyping for Southerners as well. Those with a great deal of interregional experience were less likely to stereotype Northerners than those with only an intermediate amount, although both groups were more likely to stereotype than those with little or no exposure to non-Southerners.

Wood's study was based on small convenience samples of students from two universities, and her measures were less than ideal, but if her results can be trusted, one way of reconciling them with each other, with Triandis' research, and with the usual results of research on the contact hypothesis is to assume that *no* generalization will do justice to the facts of group difference, that all will be inaccurate to some extent. Unless group differences are so large that nearly all members of one group differ from nearly all of another in the same ways (a situation that almost certainly does not exist for any two groups in the United States), we may suppose that once an individual has arrived at a generalized representation—a stereotype—of some group, whether the

2. This may be rather hard to believe, given the preponderance of Northern, or at least non-Southern, characters in the literature and mass media of the United States, but it appears that these characters, unlike Southern characters, are not seen as representative regional types, even by Southerners. If this analysis is correct, we have here an exception to the general rule that minority consciousness emerges earlier and is more salient than majority consciousness, assuming that Southerners are to be regarded as the minority in this situation.

stereotype is a normative one acquired through socialization or a non-normative one inferred from his experience, *additional* contact with members of the group will weaken and differentiate that stereotype by exposing the individual to exceptions. Cultural differences may exist between two groups, in other words, and interaction may at first produce awareness that they exist, but if there is significant overlap between the two groups, interaction should eventually begin to reduce stereotyping. It may be that even American whites who have never interacted with blacks have some preconceptions of the differences between blacks and whites in the United States; that most American gentiles (at least most of those likely to turn up in studies of Jewish-gentile relations) already have some expectations about the differences between themselves and Jews; and that nearly all non-Southern college students (if not nearly all of the general non-Southern population) have some ideas about what Southerners look like even before they actually meet any. For all these groups, the effect of contact is to undermine these normative stereotypes. But if we can believe Wood's sample of college students, Southerners who have not had any experience with non-Southerners may not have any idea, right or wrong, about how Northerners differ from their own group. The initial effect of interacting with non-Southerners is to produce working generalizations—nonnormative stereotypes—about the nature of regional differences. Only later do the inadequacies of those generalizations become apparent.

Effects of Exposure on Perceptions of Regional Differences

All of this speculation rests on the assumption that Wood's findings are reliable, but the assumption seems to be correct. Using a much larger sample, based on those white members of the general population of North Carolina who identify themselves as Southerners, and using measures somewhat different from those Wood used, we found exactly the same relationship she did between exposure to non-Southerners and regional stereotyping.

Figure 5 shows the relation between indices designed to measure those variables. The exposure variable has four values, as follows:
1. *Never been outside South*: Southern-born; never lived outside eleven Confederate States, Kentucky, and Oklahoma; longest dis-

Figure 5.   Relation of Stereotyping to Exposure

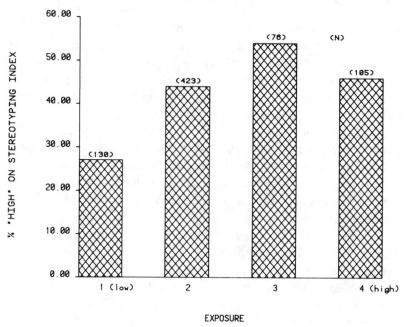

tance traveled from present home is less than five hundred miles.

2. *Traveled in North*: Southern-born, never lived outside South, long-est distance traveled is over five hundred miles. (Note: This travel may, for some respondents, have been entirely in the South. It is impossible to tell from the survey items available.)

3. *Lived in North*: Southern- or border-state-born, lived up to six years outside South (unless included in 4, below).

4. *Extensive exposure to North*: born in North, or one or more years of schooling in North, or lived in North more than six years.

This measure of exposure is somewhat rough-and-ready, but the four categories will almost certainly isolate groups of individuals with, on the average, increasing degrees of exposure to non-Southerners, and any built-in error will operate to reduce the apparent effects of such exposure. A more troublesome problem, which can only be indicated, is that the nature of the interaction cannot be specified with any precision. There is also, as Williams has pointed out, the problem of causal direction, particularly when we examine the effects of exposure on hostility; presumably, those who dislike non-Southerners will tend to avoid them. It is less clear how self-selection would affect the relation between exposure and stereotyping.

The index of stereotyping was developed from adjectives presented to respondents as follows: "Now I'm going to read some words that people use to describe other people. I'm going to ask you whether each word applies more to Northerners or to Southerners. Do you think ——applies more to Northerners or to Southerners?" The list included ten adjectives from the Katz and Braley inventory, chosen on the basis of pretesting that revealed widespread perceptions of regional differences in those respects. Courteous, religious, patriotic, slow, generous, and loyal to family are often seen as Southern traits, their opposites being, by implication, at least, Northern traits. Aggressive, industrious, materialistic, and sophisticated are traits likely to be ascribed by Southerners to Northerners. Interviewers were supplied with lists of synonyms, where pretesting indicated that an adjective's meaning might not be clear to many respondents. For each item, the stereotypic response was scored 2, responses of "no difference" and "don't know" were scored 1, and counter-stereotypic responses were scored 0. The index was trichotomized for use in this analysis by cuts between 12 and 13 and between 15 and 16. Persons scoring high on the index, then, gave the stereotypic response to the majority of items.[3]

As Figure 5 shows, Southerners who have lived a while in the North are much more likely to exhibit conventional beliefs about American regional differences than those who have never left the South; they are twice as likely to score high on the index of stereotyping. Among those who have never left the South, only 27 percent score high on the index. Forty-four percent of those who may have traveled outside the region, but have not lived outside, score high. And a majority—57 percent—of those who have lived outside the South also score high.

---

3. Stereotypical responses to one item tend to be correlated with stereotypical responses to others, although not strongly. The 45 interitem tau-b's (a measure of association ranging from 0 to 1) range from − .04 (industrious-patriotic) to .63 (religious-loyal to family), with an average around .20.

A predicted inverse U-shaped function is amiably consistent with almost any observed pattern in the data, since, after the fact, the analyst can always claim to have observed only a limited range of the independent variable. In this case, fortunately, it is not necessary to fall back to that position: the expected decline does set in for the group with the most extensive exposure to non-Southerners. In other words, these data replicate perfectly Wood's finding, based on a different population and using quite different measures. Those with an intermediate amount of interregional experience are the most likely to generalize about regional differences.

This inverse U-shaped curve appears to hold whether the generalization is a flattering one or derogatory. If we take each of the components of the stereotyping index separately and examine its relation to exposure, seven of the ten show the same curvilinear relation as the aggregate index (although, of course, these are not independent tests, and for one of the seven—perception of Southerners as more generous than Northerners—the pattern is very attenuated). One of the items—Southerners more loyal to family—is essentially unrelated to exposure, but the remaining two—Northerners more sophisticated, Southerners more courteous—have monotonic positive relations to exposure.

For nine of the ten items, in other words, exposure to non-Southerners (up to a point, at least) increases the likelihood that a Southerner will express conventionally stereotyped views of regional differences, regardless of whether the view feeds his self-esteem or not—as we would expect, if the stereotype reflects real regional differences.

Education is also positively related to regional stereotyping (tau-b = .15), suggesting that there are other ways to learn regional stereotypes than from interaction with non-Southerners. Poorly traveled Southerners with some college education are as likely to stereotype as well-traveled Southerners who are not high school graduates. Here again, we have a difference from the usual finding with regard to ethnic stereotypes; education generally seems to reduce the expression of stereotypical views of racial and ethnic groups. Education is also positively related to our index of exposure (tau-b = .26), but within each educational category, the inverse U-shaped relation between exposure and stereotyping holds up.

Relation of Cognition to Affect

Does holding stereotyped and generally unflattering views of Northerners lead Southerners to express dislike and social distance? Unfortunately, the survey did not include very good measures of sectional hostility, but responses to three items can be combined to give an index that captures several aspects of anti-Northern prejudice. The three items, with seven responses ranging from "strongly agree" to "strongly disagree," are: 1) "I don't like to hear a person with a Northern accent," 2) "Marriages between Northerners and Southerners are just as happy as marriages where both people come from the same part of the country" (scored negatively), and 3) "People who move to the South from the North never really become Southerners."[4]

The relation of the resulting index (trichotomized) to the index of stereotyping is shown in Table 9. The two indices are positively associated, but the association is negligible (tau-b = .03). The association remains positive but very small for a great many different social and demographic subgroups within the sample. Only for those respondents with at least some college education is there an association worth mentioning between stereotyping per se and prejudice (tau-b = .18), an example perhaps of the general proposition that educated people display more ideological consistency (as judged by other educated people, *i.e.*, social researchers).

In general, what this lack of association means is that simple recognition of difference does not itself imply hostility. Obviously, what the perceived difference *is* has something to do with it, and Table 10, which shows the separate association of each of the stereotype items with the hostility index, suggests that some perceived differences do affect one's feelings, while others do not. Seeing Northerners as less courteous, more aggressive, more sophisticated, more materialistic, less slow—all these perceptions have relatively little to do with how one feels toward them. But seeing them as less religious, less patriotic, less loyal to family, or less generous tends to be associated with nega-

4. The three items were only modestly related to one another, but each was related in the same way to the exposure and stereotyping variables, as were several other items that might be taken as indicators of sectional prejudice (e.g., response to a hypothetical hiring situation).

Table 9.   Score on Prejudice Index, by Score on Stereotyping Index

	Stereotyping		
Prejudice	Low	Medium	High
Low	25%	23%	25%
Medium	36	31	28
High	40	45	47
TOTAL	100%*	99%*	100%
	(168)	(239)	(306)

*Total differs from 100% due to rounding error.

Table 10.   Association (tau-b) of Stereotypic Responses with Anti-
Northern Prejudice

Response	Association
Southerners more loyal to family	.17
Southerners more generous	.10
Southerners more patriotic	.10
Southerners more religious	.10
Southerners more courteous	.01
Southerners slower	.02
Northerners more materialistic	.005
Northerners more sophisticated	−.004
Northerners more aggressive	−.06
Northerners more industrious	−.10

tive feelings toward them, while seeing them as more industrious is weakly associated with positive feelings. It is apparently quite possible to assert that there are some differences without holding that fact against the outgroup, and the Southern stereotype of Northerners includes at least one attribute—industry—that Southerners find admirable.

Return of the Contact Hypothesis

These findings should make us somewhat cautious about predicting the relationship between exposure and hostility. Although, up to a rather advanced point, stereotyping increases with interregional contact, stereotyping does not seem to have much to do with sectional prejudice. And, as Figure 6 shows, the two variables are related quite differently to our exposure index. The group scoring highest on expressions of prejudice is the group that scored lowest on the measure of stereotyping—those with little or no interregional experience. Education is also negatively related to prejudice. (Controls for it reduce the association between prejudice and exposure only slightly, however, from a tau-b of .18 to tau-b's of .12 to .17.)

In other words, the same sorts of experience—exposure to non-Southerners and education—that increase stereotyping actually seem

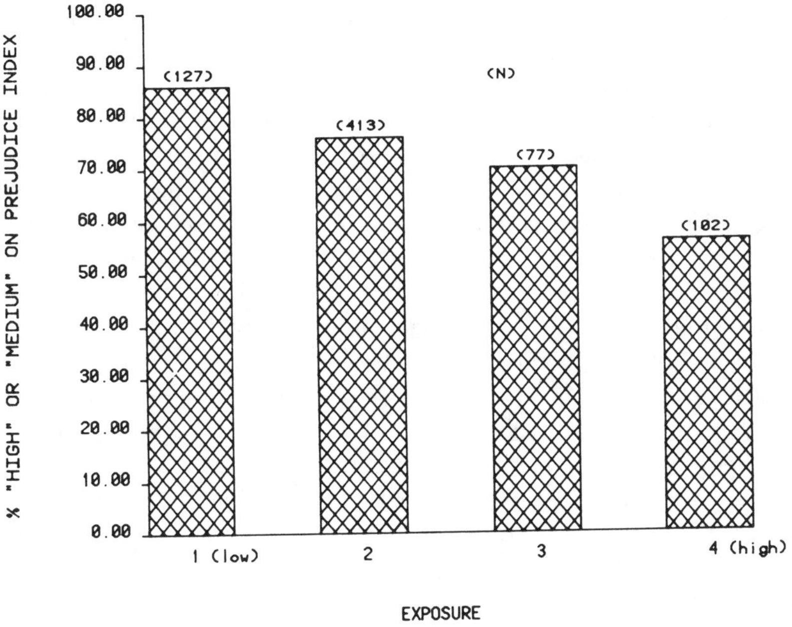

Figure 6.   Relation of Anti-Northern Prejudice to Exposure

to reduce sectional animosity. Among those Southerners with little firsthand experience outside the South, and little secondhand "experience" through education, we frequently find an inability to tell us much about Northerners, but within the same group (although not necessarily among the same individuals) we find many who view Northerners with suspicion and distrust—disliking their accents, believing Southerners should not marry them, feeling that those who move to the South will not become Southerners. This group may not know much about Northerners, but it knows what it dislikes. Those with more experience or more education are much more willing to generalize about Northerners—to compliment their industry and criticize their manners, among other things. But interregional experience and education also lead Southerners to be more tolerant of Northern accents, to have fewer reservations about regional intermarriage, and to be less likely to believe that Northern migrants are unassimilable.

It is not the case that stereotyping itself reduces hostility; the evidence is, if anything, to the contrary, especially with education and exposure controlled. But it is not the case either that interaction breaks down conventional stereotypes and thereby reduces hostility. The contact hypothesis works, after a fashion, but it works through some other mechanism than that.

What might this other mechanism be? In the absence of other data, one can only speculate, but it seems possible that interaction produces cognitive change of a sort we have not measured—change of a sort that is linked more closely to regional hostility than the changes we have measured. Could it not be that the element of predictability emphasized by Walter Lippmann in his original discussion of stereotyping, in *Public Opinion* over fifty years ago, is the missing link between interaction and affect? A known quantity, even a mildly unpleasant one, may be preferable to an unknown and unpredictable one. It seems likely that the same experiences that lead many Southerners to see Northerners as ill mannered, industrious, and the rest, make them and others less likely to see Northerners as inscrutable and possibly dangerous, thereby more than offsetting the negative effects of the stereotype. This is at least a possible explanation of a somewhat anomalous, but apparently reliable, set of findings.

III. Southernness at the Margins

7. Shalom, Y'All
Jewish Southerners

We seldom think of ethnic diversity as a characteristic of the American South. In his presidential address to the Southern Historical Association, George Tindall characterized his region as "the biggest single WASP nest this side of the Atlantic," and certainly the region's non-British ethnic groups (leaving its blacks aside, as usual) have been small—as Southern chambers of commerce used to remind us. But they haven't been few. Tindall quoted a South Carolina historian, writing in 1809: "So many and so various have been the sources from which Carolina has derived her population, that a considerable period must elapse, before the people amalgamate into a mass possessing a uniform national character." And Tindall observed:

> [Although] a considerable period has elapsed . . . there are still those exceptions which prove the rule: a few reminders of forgotten Spaniards and Frenchmen, some Mexican-Americans renamed Chicanos, some Cuban cigar-makers and the more recent Cuban refugees, some German counties out in Texas, Cajuns up the bayous, Italians in New Orleans, Hungarians over in Tangipahoa Parish, a scattering of Czechs, Dutch, Ukrainians, and in Mississippi, even Chinese. Jews are visible, if scarce, in most localities; politicians in Charleston used to reckon with the Irish and Germans; and there are those enclaves of mixed-blood Lumbees, Tuscaroras, "Brass Ankles," Melungeons, and Turks, not to mention remnants of Cherokees, Catawbas, Creeks, and Seminoles.

These Southern ethnic groups have not been totally ignored by social scientists—John Maclachlan called attention to them in a 1939 *Social Forces* article and, more recently, Kenneth Morland edited a volume called *The Not So Solid South*—but we have yet to realize the contribution that the study of such groups could make to our general understanding of ethnic group relations. That realization will come, I suspect, only when we introduce an explicit comparative emphasis and ask how these groups have differed from similar groups elsewhere in the United States. There are hints, here and there in the literature, that ethnicity has somehow worked out differently in the South. For instance, Tindall speculates that the South is, "perhaps, the one part of the country where the melting pot really worked, because so few ingredients were added after independence. . . . Over the years all those Southerners with names like Kruttschnitt, Kolb, DeBardeleben, Huger, Lanneau, Toledano, Moise, Jastremski, or Cheros got melted down and poured back out in the mold of good old boys and girls, if not of the gentry. Who, for example, could be more WASPish than Scarlett O'Hara, in more ways than one?" Whether Tindall's hunch is correct is less important than the point that we might want to test our generalizations about American ethnic groups in the context of "Uncle Sam's other province" (as Allen Tate called the South). The ties that bind Southerners, like those that hold ethnic groups together, are "primordial" (in Edward Shils's term), and Southernism may interact and compete with ethnic identification and ethnic culture in ways that Americanism does not. If the Southern outcome has been different, we may learn something important about the South and about American ethnic groups. At the very least, ethnic identification in the South has produced some colorful hybrids, like the Irish of Savannah, who celebrate Saint Patrick's Day with a breakfast including green grits.

All of this suggests an ambitious program of research. Here I am reporting just a preliminary and modest (to put it no more apologetically) contribution to that program, an attempt to use secondary analysis of national sample surveys to study some aspects of the acculturation of Southern Jews.

Jews in the South

Outside an Armenian merchant's shop in the Old City of Jerusalem hangs a ceramic plaque that says "Shalom, Y'all." That shopkeeper evidently knows something we often overlook—that a lot of Jews live in the South. Nearly half a million do, in fact, giving the South a Jewish population larger than those of all but five nations in the world. But if Southern Jews are not exactly few, they are certainly far between. Out of every 1000 Americans, about 260 live in the South

and about 30 are Jewish, but only 2 are Jews who live in the South—
and one of those lives in Florida, which hardly counts.[1]

This may be one reason why "[t]he literature on southern Jews is
thin" (as Leonard Dinnerstein and Mary Dale Palsson remark in their
edited volume, *Jews in the South*). To study Southern Jews, it appears,
you have to intend to study them; most students of American Jewry
have neglected the 7 percent who are Southerners, and most students
of the South ignore the fraction of 1 percent of the population who are
Jewish. Even if one sets out specifically to study Southern Jews, the
task is not an easy one; there are some daunting methodological problems involved in locating a representative sample to study. Thus, what
literature we have was characterized by Alfred Hero as "a handful of
biographies, autobiographies, and historical works (mostly of dubious
quality), and the results of interviews in several Southern Jewish communities." Until recently we have lacked even a simple demographic
description of Southern Jewry as a whole, and discussions of the attitudes, values, and behaviors of Southern Jews have rested on informed
surmise or extrapolations from studies of a few, perhaps atypical, communities.

The way in which those attitudes, values, and behaviors have been
influenced by the Southern environment is not clear. In *White Southerners*, Lewis Killian observes that many Southerners of both races
see Southern Jews as at least potentially "different," particularly with
regard to their racial attitudes. On the other hand, most social scientists
who have studied them emphasize, usually disapprovingly, their acculturation. As Dinnerstein and Palsson summarize the literature, "Except for different religious practices, [Southern] Jews made every effort
to become absorbed into the activities of their adopted home. Their
life-style closely resembled that of their gentile neighbors." Almost certainly either extreme view is an oversimplification, and I shall examine
some other possibilities, but the point is that we have no basis for assuming much of anything about what Southern Jews believe, in the
aggregate, or how they behave.

1. These statistics are taken from data collected by the American Jewish Committee,
American Jewish Year Book, 1970 (Philadelphia: Jewish Publication Society of
America, 1970), LXXI, 345–46. "The South" here refers to the eleven ex-
Confederate states, Kentucky, and Oklahoma.

In order to examine those questions directly, I constructed a sample of 166 Southern Jews, by pooling the data from fifty-six Gallup Polls conducted between November, 1968, and November, 1972.[2] While any conclusions based on these data must obviously be very tentative, at least the shortcomings of this method are rather different from those inherent in previous studies of Southern Jews, and perhaps these data will complement theirs. The great advantage of this pooled sample is that it appears to be geographically representative of the total population of Southern Jews, and there are reasons to suppose that it is representative in other respects as well. And although the sample size is still quite small, it is comparable to those employed in many community studies.

Since the data come from many Gallup Polls, we must restrict our inquiry to those subjects about which questions were asked on at least most of the separate surveys. Even so, we can extract some information on three topics: 1) the demographic characteristics of Southern Jews, 2) their political behavior, and 3) their participation in organized religious life.

Demographic Characteristics

When the results of the National Jewish Population Study are available, we will have a demographic description of Southern Jewry far superior to anything this small sample can give us. In the meantime, however, it may be worthwhile to summarize the description that emerges from these data. If we leave the Floridians aside, Southern Jews, on the average, are an urban population (roughly two-thirds live in cities larger than 250,000); well educated (a majority have at least some college education); concentrated in professional, managerial, and executive occupations (about half of the heads of households are in these categories, perhaps one in eight is a skilled or unskilled worker, and the balance are clerical or sales workers or retired); and, in conse-

---

2. The data were obtained from the Roper Center for Public Opinion Research, and the cooperation of the center and its staff is gratefully acknowledged. I discussed the sample and its problems in an article called "Needles in Haystacks," in the *Public Opinion Quarterly*.

quence, economically well off (median reported income—*ca.* 1970— was between $10,000 and $11,000). Compared to non-Southern American Jews, they seem to be somewhat better educated, on the average, but the two groups have virtually the same occupational and age distributions. The regional environment of Southern Jews may be reflected in their median income (which is lower than that for non-Southern Jews) and in the fact that fewer live in large cities and somewhat more—perhaps one in eight—in rural areas and towns under 50,000 population. The Jews of Florida, on the average, are older and have lower incomes than either non-Southern or other Southern Jews, and their educational distribution looks about like that for the former group.

One implication of these data is that the attitudes and behavior of Southern Jews should be compared not to those of the white Southern population as a whole, but rather to those of middle-class, urban Southern whites—the ones they might reasonably be expected to resemble. I have attempted below to introduce a rough control for this difference.

Voting Behavior

Most of the Gallup Polls that were pooled to yield this sample asked how their respondents voted in the 1968 presidential election. Seventy-nine of the 166 in the sample were asked the question, had voted in 1968, and recalled how they voted. While we cannot, with these data, explore Southern Jews' political views in any depth, this single indicator has much to commend it as a measure of general political orientation. A vote for Hubert Humphrey can probably be taken without much error to indicate center-to-left views; a vote for Richard Nixon, center-to-right views; and (in the South) a vote for George Wallace of Alabama was highly correlated with a whole array of culturally conservative attitudes (including, but by no means limited to, support for racial segregation), which Harold Grasmick, a student of the Wallace movement, has labeled *the* "traditional [Southern] value orientation."

Certainly 1968 was an election .n which the voting behavior of white Southerners generally differed greatly from that of most American

Jews.[3] Jewish voters went for Humphrey, the Democrat, by nearly four to one over Nixon, and virtually ignored the Wallace candidacy. White Southern voters, on the other hand, gave Nixon twice as many votes as Humphrey (who got only one vote in five), and gave Wallace nearly as many votes as Nixon. Even among college-educated white Southerners, Wallace took one vote in five and Humphrey only one in four. Few population groups in the country were more clearly on opposite sides in that election than American Jews and Southern whites, which leads to the obvious question, How did Southern Jews, who belong to both groups, resolve these cross-pressures?

There are some reasons, in principle, to suppose that Southern Jews will look pretty much like their non-Southern coreligionists, that is, unlike their fellow white Southerners. As Seymour Martin Lipset summarizes the evidence, "All studies of Jewish political opinion agree that the *social-class* factors which strongly divide non-Jews on political lines . . . have little effect on the views or party choices of Jews [emphasis added]." Herbert Hyman comments, "To use an old-fashioned term, the membership characteristic 'Jewish' is 'prepotent'—it overrides class membership." Perhaps one could argue that if it can wash out the effects of social class, that powerful predictor of political behavior, surely it can override the effects of region as well.

On the other hand, as we saw earlier, some of the literature on Southern Jews has remarked their acculturation to the folkways of the white South. George Maddox has implied as much by noting "surface indications that Jews have been fairly well integrated into predominantly Gentile communities within the region," while observing that "this acceptance depends on continuous public manifestations of accommodation by Jews, whatever their private opinions, to the regional culture, especially in regard to race relationships." Lewis Killian argues

3.   The figures for white voters in this paragraph and in Tables 11 and 12 were computed from data in Norval Glenn, "Class and Party Support in the United States: Recent and Emerging Trends," in the *Public Opinion Quarterly*, for white respondents, ages 21 to 59, to several Gallup Polls. Those for middle-class white voters were computed from Glenn's tables for respondents with at least some college education. The figures for non-Southern Jewish voters are based on 159 respondents to AIPO (Gallup Poll) studies 779, 783, 789, 793, and 801. Both for Southern and non-Southern Jews, I used weights for "at-homeness" supplied by the Gallup Organization, although these weights in fact made very little difference in the resulting percentages.

that the marginality of Southern Jews "has placed a high premium on conformity to the regional mores," and that, whatever the level of anti-Semitism in the South, "there has been *enough* latent anti-Semitism . . . to make good southerners out of many Jews." Whether this alleged conformity to Southern ways is internalized or only a sort of protective coloration, this view suggests that the political views Southern Jews express (including those they express to Gallup Poll interviewers) should resemble the views of their white neighbors.

Obviously, we should not expect either extreme outcome—complete similarity to non-Southern Jews or to other Southern whites. There are good reasons to suppose that degree of acculturation is greatly variable, certainly from one community to another, and even within specific Southern towns, where (Theodor Lowi argued in the Dinnerstein and Palsson volume) it serves as a basis for stratification within the Jewish community. Moreover, Southern Jews should be compared not to the aggregate of Southern whites, but rather to other Southern whites with similar demographic and economic characteristics.

In fact, as Table 11 shows, Southern Jewish voters did exhibit a level of support for Hubert Humphrey intermediate between that of non-Southern Jews and that of middle-class Southern whites generally. (The vote distribution of Jews from Florida was practically identical to that for other Southern Jews, so I have reported the aggregate figure here. Neither of the two Wallace voters was from Florida.) Although in this respect Southern Jews look somewhat more like other American Jews than like other middle-class Southerners, the effect of region is by no means obliterated among Jews; it is substantial, and at least as great as the regional effect found among middle-class voters in general. Put another way, the difference between Jews and middle-class white voters generally is no larger in the South than elsewhere in the United States—and not much smaller either. The effects of region and of religion are roughly additive, although those of religion are substantially larger.

This generalization does not hold, however, when we look at support for George Wallace. Although Southern Jews were twice as likely as non-Southern Jews to vote against Humphrey in 1968, their votes went to Nixon, not to the Wallace third party (Table 12). Wallace received 37 percent of the votes of Southern whites, about half that fraction of the middle-class white vote, but only a minuscule proportion of

Table 11. Vote for Hubert Humphrey, 1968, by Region, for Jews
and for Middle-Class White Voters Generally

| | Percentage for Humphrey | | |
	Jewish voters	Middle-class white voters	(Difference)
South	59%	24%	(35)
Non-South	79%	39%	(40)
(Difference)	(20)	(15)	

Table 12. Vote for George Wallace, 1968, by Region, for Jews and
for Middle-Class White Voters Generally

| | Percentage for Wallace | | |
	Jewish voters	Middle-class white voters	(Difference)
South	3%	18%	(15)
Non-South	1%	1%	(——)
(Difference)	(2)	(17)	

the votes of Jewish Southerners. In this respect, Southern Jews resembled non-Southern Jews (and non-Southern middle-class voters
generally). We can say, if we want, that being Jewish "washed out" the
observed regional difference in support for Wallace—or, alternatively,
that only in the South was there a difference between Jews and the
total category of white middle-class voters.

To judge by this single indicator, then, Southern Jews do show the
effects of their regional environment. If a Nixon vote in 1968 can be
taken to indicate conservatism, they are more conservative than non-
Southern Jews—to about the same extent that middle-class white
Southerners in general are more conservative than non-Southern
middle-class whites. But their acculturation has not been so great as to
blot out their differences from Southern gentiles, or to lure them into
the Wallace camp in any significant number.

Attendance at Religious Services

One of the persisting differences between Southern and non-Southern white Protestants has been that the former are more likely to belong to a church and to attend its services. Many observers of the South have commented on the subtle and not-so-subtle pressures to adhere at least nominally to some church, almost without regard to which. Just how this pressure is experienced by Southern Jews is not clear, but they may feel more obliged than non-Southern Jews to define themselves as *something*, religiously, by active membership in a religious congregation.

There is, in addition, the effect of living as a very small minority in a population composed almost entirely of Evangelical Protestants. Although this fact, and the sometimes-documented anti-Jewish sentiment of many Southern Protestants, may make Jewish religious life more difficult, it may also increase the need for it, among those who continue to define themselves as Jewish.

Perhaps it is not surprising, then, to find that the Southern Jews in our sample (excluding those from Florida, who look in this respect like non-Southern Jews) are relatively likely to answer affirmatively when asked by a Gallup interviewer, "Did you, yourself, happen to attend church [*sic*] in the last seven days?" Of the 61 respondents not from Florida who were asked the question, 35 percent said they had, compared to an average figure for the total United States Jewish population of 19 to 20 percent. This regional difference is at least as large as that reported elsewhere for white Protestants. (In both South and non-South—perhaps especially in the latter—Jews are somewhat less likely than white Protestants to report attendance. Here again, the effects of region and religion are roughly additive.)

Notice that acculturation has a novel twist in this respect. By being more Southern—that is, by participating in organized religious activities—Southern Jews are at the same time more Jewish. I suspect that many other suggestive anomalies are there to be found by students of group life in the South.

Limitations and a Suggestion

The limitations of these data are painfully obvious to me, as I assume they are to most readers. I have discussed elsewhere some of the problems with the sample, not least of which is simply its size (particularly when Floridians are excluded), which effectively precludes analysis of variations within the Southern Jewish population. Certainly there must be such variations. Presumably Jews in large Southern cities with large Jewish populations display different patterns of accommodation than Jews who live isolated in small towns with one, two, or a half-dozen Jewish families and no Jewish communal or congregational life to speak of. A larger sample would let us paint a more detailed picture.

Another shortcoming, again an obvious one, is that we have no way of distinguishing recent migrants to the South from longtime residents. Indeed, we cannot even estimate, at this writing, what proportion each is of the population. The presence of this factor probably exaggerates the apparent differences between Jewish and non-Jewish Southerners (and the similarity between Southern and non-Southern Jews), but there is no way to estimate the magnitude of the exaggeration.

Finally, it would be delightful if it were possible to inquire about a wider range of acculturation variables, using better measures than the Gallup Poll (conducted for entirely different purposes) yields. The nature of the pooling operation that produced the sample leads to lowest-common-denominator dependent variables, and there is nothing to be done about that.

Maybe, however, this tentative (and inexpensive) venture in secondary analysis will serve to suggest that there are some interesting, important, and unanswered questions about Jews in the South, questions deserving the attention that could be given them by primary analysis, that is, by research undertaken specifically to answer them. I hope it will also suggest the more general possibilities of ethnic group research in a comparative regional framework.

8. Blacks and Southerners

(with Merle Black)

The Negro in the South," wrote the historian L. D. Reddick in 1960, "is a study in attachment and alienation. For him, identification has always been a problem. Inescapably he has found himself to be a 'Southerner.' He may not have preferred the term, but the objective fact could not be denied." Reddick observed that "the conflict between embracing and rejecting the South" is resolved in different ways. "Some [black Southerners] hate the South; others, despite everything, love it. Most, however, alternate their love and hate, while a few seem to be capable of loving and hating at the same time. It is a great and confusing frustration."

To our knowledge, no one has undertaken systematic and empirical study of this troubled relationship (an omission that would be more surprising if more attention had been paid to the regional attitudes of *white* Americans). To be sure, here and there, black Southern writers and politicians have begun to explore their roots in the South, usually displaying in the process the localism and sense of place for which their white fellow-Southerners are often noted. In *South to a Very Old Place*, Albert Murray has given us a remarkable book on the subject, and most symposium volumes on the South now contain contributions from black Southerners. (Among the most interesting are the essays by Louis Lomax and Arna Bontemps in *The South Today*, edited by Willie Morris, and Don Anderson's contribution to a 1981 "neo-Agrarian" manifesto, *Why the South Will Survive*.) For the most part, however, our information about the attitudes of ordinary black Southerners has come from journalistic narrative or from rather risky inference—the "foot-votes" of black migration statistics, for instance. If, as these statistics suggest, blacks' attitudes toward the South are changing, a study of those attitudes may be particularly timely. In the course of such a study, we came across some data striking enough to be reported in this abbreviated and preliminary form.

Since 1964, each presidential election study by the University of Michigan has included a series of questions asking respondents to rate several politically relevant groups on a "feeling thermometer," ranging from 0 (cold) through 50 (indifferent) to 100 (warm). One of the groups respondents have been asked to rate is Southerners. Figure 7 shows for each of four groups—Southern and non-Southern blacks and whites—the percentage in each year who gave a "warm" rating (51–100) to Southerners.[1]

In each year, for both races, there are substantial regional differences in this proportion. Not surprisingly, Southern whites have warmer feelings toward Southerners than do non-Southern whites; Southern blacks, for their part, feel warmer toward Southerners than do non-Southern blacks. These regional differences show no appreciable diminution during the twelve-year period.

At the beginning of the period, large racial differences were also evident, about the same magnitude as the regional differences. Southern blacks' ratings were substantially cooler than those of Southern whites, roughly the same as those of non-Southern whites. Non-Southern blacks' attitudes in 1964 were, on the average, positively frosty; 45 percent rated Southerners at 49 or below, while only 27 percent felt at all warm toward them (the balance were indifferent).

By the mid-1970s, however, the gap between blacks' and whites' ratings had closed in the South, and outside the region had even been reversed. Southern blacks were as likely as Southern whites—very likely—to express warmth toward Southerners, while non-Southern blacks had warmed up in an equally dramatic fashion. By 1976 a solid 57 percent rated their feelings as warm, a higher proportion than that of non-Southern whites, who lapsed back into tepidity after a temporary surge of goodwill in the early 1970s.

These findings are paralleled by the results of another question asked by the Michigan survey in 1976. Respondents were shown a list

1. Except for non-Southern blacks before 1972, the majority of respondents who did not give Southerners a warm rating registered indifference, not hostility. The South as defined by the survey organization comprises ten of the eleven ex-Confederate states. Tennessee is excluded, apparently because it is too Republican.

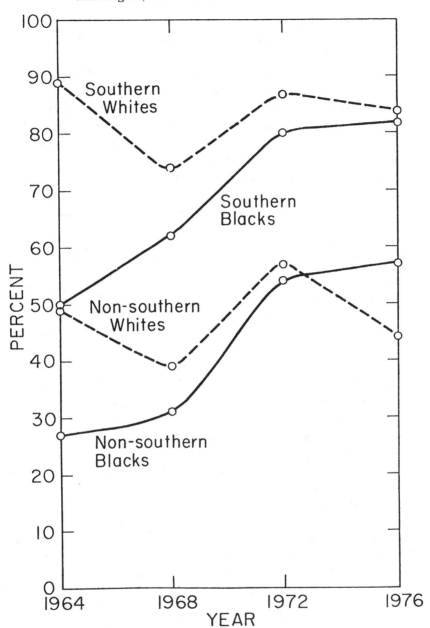

Figure 7. Percent Who Feel "Warm" Toward Southerners, by Race and Region, 1964–1976

of groups and then asked if they felt "close to" any of the groups, including Southerners, whites, and blacks. Within the South, the percentages of whites and of blacks expressing "closeness" to Southerners were similar—43 percent of whites and 39 percent of blacks. Among non-Southerners, though, blacks were three times as likely as whites to indicate closeness to Southerners (30 percent, versus 10 percent).

Presenting these figures is one thing, and interpreting them, of course, quite another. We sought, without conspicuous success, to locate these changes within the black population, that is, to find subpopulations that have changed faster or slower than others. But the change has been strikingly uniform across age, education, and size-of-place categories within both the Southern and non-Southern black populations. Only for small-town Southern blacks has the change been at all retarded (they show, in fact, very little change at all), but they started out with much warmer feelings toward Southerners than did urban Southern blacks; by 1976, the latter had simply caught up.

These trends in black public opinion obviously reflect social and political changes in the South since the mid-1960s. Confronted historically with extensive racial discrimination in the legal system, education, employment, and housing, pervasive segregation in places of public accommodations, and widespread exclusion from the region's political system, many Southern blacks dissented from the white supremacist values embedded in the traditional "Southern way of life." The civil rights movement, resulting federal legislation, and the general acquiescence of Southern whites to the desegregation of public accommodations and the extension of the franchise have enabled Southern blacks to enter into more nearly full citizenship. We suggest that Southern blacks have responded both by reevaluating their white fellow Southerners and by laying claim themselves to the label *Southerner.*

While we cannot directly demonstrate that black Southerners have become more favorably inclined toward white Southerners—the symbol needed for a definitive answer never appeared in the surveys—we can show that Southern blacks have become warmer toward whites as a group and that their evaluations of whites have continued to be positively associated with their evaluations of Southerners. In 1964, only a slight majority (55 percent) of black Southerners responded warmly to whites. By 1976, almost 80 percent did so. (The correlation of

Southern blacks' thermometer ratings of whites and Southerners was .45 in 1964 and .36 in 1976.) Our inference is that white Southerners were more favorably evaluated by black Southerners in the 1970s (although considerable social distance remained, since only one-fifth of black Southerners reported feeling *close* to whites).

This reevaluation of Southern whites is important, but we suggest that an explanation of these trends in black public opinion may lie as much in a change in the referent of the word *Southerners* as in changed feelings toward a constant referent. In 1964, we suspect, many Southern blacks may have been unclear about whether the category was meant to include them and their black friends and neighbors. (If they did understand it to include them, they were evidently not pleased with some of the company their inclusion placed them in.) The survey data support this interpretation, showing virtually no relationship in 1964 between black Southerners' feelings toward blacks and their evaluation of Southerners ($r = .08$). Twelve years later, however, a modest correlation ($r = .35$) had emerged. By the 1970s, it appears, many Southern blacks did understand themselves to be Southerners, and they were not unhappy about that fact.

Fred Powledge, a perceptive Southern-bred journalist, wrote in his book *Journeys Through the South*: "I would wager that if anybody asked them, black people from or living in the South would respond that they think of themselves as Southerners. Maybe they don't use the term as frequently as whites. Maybe they are preoccupied—because the rest of society has for so long been preoccupied—with their being blacks first. But I have never seen or heard a black Southerner wince or groan or complain when I referred to him or her as a 'Southerner.'" And Powledge is right; in 1971, a sample of the adult general population of North Carolina was asked this question: "Some people around here think of themselves as Southerners, others do not. How about you—would you say that you are a Southerner or not?" Seventy-five of the black respondents allowed that they were Southerners, only slightly fewer than the 82 percent of white respondents who did so.

If non-Southern blacks also take the word *Southerner* to include Southern blacks, this may explain the fact that they feel warmer toward Southerners (and "closer" to them) than do non-Southern whites. They are more likely than non-Southern whites to be themselves migrants from the South (and migrants of both races feel warmer toward the South than do non-Southern natives), and they are presumably more likely to be linked to the region by ties of friendship and kinship.

Our data persuade us not only that black Americans now regard Southern blacks as Southerners but that they are less ambivalent about this identification than they were just a few years ago. An important final question, about which we have little evidence, is what the referent of *Southerner* is for white Americans, particularly for white Southerners. The available evidence suggests that white Southerners have changed their feelings far less than black Southerners. The percentage of white Southerners reporting warm feelings toward blacks did *not* increase from 1964 to 1976; in the mid-1970s, only a slim majority of white Southerners (51 percent) felt favorably disposed towards blacks, compared to 55 percent in the mid-1960s. Only a minuscule 5 percent of Southern whites volunteered that they felt "close" to blacks. Finally, only in 1972 and 1976 did even a trace of association ($r = .14$ and $.12$, respectively) emerge among whites in the South between their feelings toward Southerners and their evaluation of blacks. We suspect that "Southerner" still primarily means *white* Southerner for most of the region's dominant racial group, although many Southern whites would, on second thought, probably allow that Southern blacks are indeed Southerners, too.

If and when Southern whites are prepared to include Southern blacks within the circle of Southerners, while retaining (as they evidently do) their high opinion of that circle, that would be a change indeed. It would be, however, no more than recognition of the fact that, as Powledge puts it, "black Southerners *are* Southerners. They are of and by and from and for the South as least as much as their white brethren, and they have repeatedly demonstrated . . . their love for and faith in the region."

9.   Grits and Gravy
The South's New Middle Class

We can learn something about Southern life in these last decades of the twentieth century from the pages of *Southern Living*. By 1981, that magazine's circulation had grown to roughly two million, which means that something like one Southern household in ten subscribed to it. Since it appeals primarily to Southerners with money to spend on food processors and second homes, it seems likely that it can be found on the coffee table of one in every three or four upper-middle-class homes in the South.[1]

The magazine's success and its "up-scale demographics" have earned it a number of awards, not to mention a great deal of money; obviously it is giving upper-middle-class Southerners something they want. I suggest that we can use the magazine to begin an ethnography of this poorly understood population, to learn something about how they spend their money and their leisure time, about what concerns them and what does not, about their ideals and aspirations.

This would be a useful enterprise, because we simply don't know much about the new urban and suburban middle class of the South. We don't even *think* we know something. The extensive repertoire of American regional stereotypes just does not include one for middle-class Southerners.

And it never has. Somewhere between the planters and their set, on the one hand, and the poor whites and poor blacks of the South, on the

1.   These estimates are my own, based on the results of a readership survey that *Southern Living* kindly made available. Unfortunately their demographic breakdowns do not include one for race, so it is probably safest to assume that my generalizations here apply only to the white Southern middle class, especially since blacks do not figure prominently in the magazine's text or advertising. The survey data I discuss below are also based on samples of Southern whites, although I would be surprised to find that different patterns hold for Southern blacks.

other, a large part of our region's population has slipped through the cracks. Scholars have paid some attention to the black and white middle classes, but our cultural mythmakers have pretty well ignored them. Their discreet charm has been overshadowed by the glamor of the upper class and by the sentimental appeal of the toiling masses.

It's instructive, for example, to consider the Carter family—not the musical one from southwest Virginia, but the political one from south Georgia. Jimmy Carter made a lot of Americans uneasy; they couldn't pigeonhole his style. His combination of professionalism and piety, of informality and rigidity, was something new to their experience. After two years of his administration, a *New Yorker* correspondent confessed: "There is something about Jimmy Carter which makes him opaque to me. . . . With [him], I am in the dark." She envied her Southern friends, who seemed to understand the man, but admitted that she felt on firmer ground with Giscard or Schmidt than with her own president (thereby confirming some of my darker suspicions about *New Yorker* correspondents, not to say New Yorkers).

Certainly Carter puzzled the Northeastern media, until he began simply to annoy them. They understood Hubert Humphrey well enough, and they made fun of him when he announced the "politics of joy," but they didn't know what to make of it when Carter promised a government of national salvation. They could not figure out what kind of man uses the pages of *Playboy* to confess to the moral equivalent of adultery, what kind of president would walk in his own parade, lecture bureaucrats about living in sin, try to convert foreign heads of state, and not serve hard liquor on state occasions (although he drank it himself in private). Carter's threat to whip Senator Kennedy's ass was a puzzle to those Yankees who didn't realize that Baptist Sunday-school teachers always talk that way about Roman Catholics.

No, this born-again Annapolis graduate, this peanut merchant and nuclear engineer, was an enigma to many people—unpredictable, and a little bit spooky. His brother was a different matter. There was already a slot for Billy, and he could fill it to perfection, if he worked at it (which he did). We know about ignorant, no 'count, rural Southern whites. Call them rednecks or call them good ol' boys, depending on whether you like them, but certainly there have been plenty of them in the literature and mass media of the United States.

And Miz Lillian was a familiar type, too—the Southern *grande dame*, the apotheosis of the belle. Even Walter Cronkite knew to fetch a chair for *her*. You shouldn't ask, though, how Miz Lillian and Billy happened to be mother and son. That juxtaposition was almost as troubling as the contradictions Brother Jimmy embodied all by himself.

The fact is, of course, that the Carters are middle-class, *upper-middle-class* Southerners, and the old stereotypes of Southerners don't fit such folks comfortably. Any moderately reflective middle-class Southern boy who has put in some time in the North can probably testify to this. He finds that he can exaggerate his good manners and live up to people's idea of the Southern gentleman, or he can learn to crush beer cans with one hand, work up some colorful down-home figures of speech, whoop and holler and raise hell a lot, and live up to another set of expectations. Neither of these roles comes with complete spontaneity, but each is easy enough for most middle-class Southern males to play, so Northerners often have their expectations confirmed. I'm told that slaves used to call a similar process "puttin' on ol' Massa."

The point is that in our national consciousness the Southern middle class is effectively invisible. But it is not invisible to the publishers of *Southern Living*, who have grasped at least the commercial implications of the fact that the urban and suburban middle class of the South is growing at a phenomenal rate. The South's economic success story over the last few decades has been made up of hundreds of thousands of individual success stories. In 1930, only 15 percent or so of the South's labor force was employed at white-collar jobs. (The rest were in agriculture or manual occupations.) By 1980, that proportion had more than trebled, and now a majority of all Southern workers are in white-collar occupations—getting and spending, buying and selling, managing and "researching" and "communicating"—which they seem to feel beats chopping cotton, and I wouldn't disagree with them.

And the fastest growth in the Southern occupational structure is taking place at the top, in the categories the census bureau calls "managers and administrators, except farm," and "professional, technical and kindred workers"—in other words, in the upper-middle class. Between 1965 and 1980 the number of people in these categories just about doubled. The South is adding 300,000 or 400,000 professional and managerial people and their families to its upper-middle class each year. By 1980, they were a quarter of the South's population.

Apparently a lot of these people celebrate their arrival by taking out a subscription to *Southern Living*, and *Southern Living* serves them well, giving them some guidance they evidently appreciate. Wherever today's upper-middle class is coming from, it cannot be, in most cases, from yesterday's upper-middle class, because that class hardly existed a few decades ago. It simply must be the case that most of these people have either moved up in the Southern social structure or moved down from the North. And whether they're newly middle class or newly Southern, they can use some instruction, some sort of how-to-do-it manual, in living the Southern good life. *Southern Living* tells them in no uncertain terms how to spend their upper-middle-class incomes appropriately.

Look at the magazine in this light sometime. You'll find articles that begin something like "Azaleas have always been a feature of Southern gardens," or "Ham is a traditional part of Southern hospitality." This is *useful* information, both for migrants who want to fit in and for Southerners whose childhood gardens ran more to tomatoes, okra, and snap beans than to azaleas and who weren't eating high enough on the hog to be anywhere near the ham.

Both components of the new middle class—socially mobile Southerners and geographically mobile non-Southerners—are interesting, and each awaits its ethnographer. Here, I want to concentrate on the South's homegrown *haute bourgeoisie*. In what respects, if any, is it still useful to think of them as Southerners? If the New South, that urban industrial society we can see taking shape around us, has become (as I believe) a middle-class society, this means the end of the South-as-we-know-it. Does it mean the end of the South, period? One of the products *Southern Living* advertises these days is a "Southerner" T-shirt, available for $5.95 mail-order from Baton Rouge. Can it be that Southernness has become something to put on at home but not to wear to work? Is it possible that you now have to read someone's shirt to know where he comes from?

To judge from *Southern Living*, some Southern traditions still persist: good eating, gardening, outdoor sports, traveling and visiting, house pride and family life. But of course the magazine and its advertisers have an interest in seeing them persist, and in these respects *Southern Living* doesn't differ much from other "shelter" publications. But there are differences. To my knowledge, no other house-and-garden magazine picks an all-star football team and publishes recipes for tail-gate parties; no other so regularly prints recipes for game; and no other has as many liquor ads—oddly, in light of what has been called the South's "Eleventh Commandment." (Traditionalists may be relieved to learn, though, that one of my students calculated that *Southern Living*'s liquor ads are significantly more likely than those in the *New Yorker* to be for bourbon.)

Maybe we can get a better line on the South's new middle class if we turn from the pages of its favorite magazine to the results of some survey research. In his unpublished dissertation, Harold Grasmick, after a review of the literature on modernization throughout the world and a painstaking statistical analysis, identified eight characteristics he called "*the* traditional value orientation" typical of folk, peasant, and village cultures and of the preindustrial parts of the South's population. The eight traits are localism, fatalism, racism, familism, authoritarianism, traditional sex-role ideology, resistance to innovation, and, in the Southern context, some aspects of sectionalism (lots of -*isms*, but you get the idea).

Grasmick demonstrates that the least *völkische* Southerners are those who 1) did not grow up on a farm, 2) did get some college education, 3) presently live in cities, 4) have traveled or lived outside the South, and 5) are frequently exposed to mass media—in other words, the new Southern middle class. In 1947, in *The Way of the South*, Howard Odum wrote that "the way of the South has been and is the way of the folk. . . . The culture of the South is the culture of the folk." To the considerable extent that he was right, the way and culture of the South do not persist among urban and suburban middle-class Southerners, who are the least Southern elements in the South's population—if by *Southern* we mean racist, localistic, authoritarian, and the rest.

Even their speech is less Southern. Some sociolinguistic research has found that this is the group most likely to have acquired the postvocalic *r*—the absence of which has heretofore marked most Southern accents. Their new precision in speech may be offset, though, by the fact that they're also the group most likely to drink (or at least to admit that they do), as the ads in *Southern Living* might suggest. There is very little difference in this respect between them and other urban, middle-class Americans.

So, to fill the stereotype gap, I offer you one of the New Southerners, returning to an urban or suburban home from a managerial or professional job, sipping bourbon while he—or she—reads *Southern Living* magazine, subvocally pronouncing the *r*'s. He may have some country cousins—probably does—and he is probably less traditional (in Grasmick's sense) than they are. He may still be different from the American mainstream, whatever that is, but he is not as different as they are, or as his parents probably were.

But this picture is incomplete. In some important ways, this cosmopolitan creature is still a Southerner. He is, for starters, more self-conscious about it. It wouldn't occur to his traditional kinfolk to wear a "Southerner" T-shirt. For that to appeal to you, you have to move in circles where Southernness is not taken for granted. We've found in some recent survey research that, for many Southerners, education, media exposure, and travel and residence in the North are "consciousness-raising experiences." The very same factors that are eliminating Southerners' village and peasant characteristics produce Southerners who *think* of themselves as Southerners, who have thought about what that means, and who are proud of their regional identity.

A reasonable question, of course, is what these self-conscious Southerners are self-conscious *about*. If their cultural distinctiveness is disappearing, the situation I'm describing sounds like the cultural equivalent of reviewing your life in the course of drowning (drowning, presumably, in the mainstream).

Well, obviously Southern culture has not been limited to the folk-culture traits that Grasmick studied. In other ways that Southerners have differed from other Americans, middle-class Southerners remain regional creatures. To summarize a lot of research very briefly, let us return to the *Southern Living* reader we last saw sitting in the den, nursing a bourbon and water. Compared to the average reader of *Sunset* or of *New York* magazine, he is much more likely to belong to a church, to support it financially, and actually to attend it. He is more orthodox in his religious beliefs. (Indeed, there is some evidence that regional differences in this respect were larger in 1980 than they had been in 1960.) He is more likely to approve of violence and to employ it, in a variety of circumstances that include his leisure-time activities, reflected in *Southern Living*'s game recipes and all-star football teams.

His politics are more conservative, in the free-enterprise sense of that word. Not only are his economic views more conservative than those of other Americans, they are more conservative now than they used to be—a fact somewhat obscured by his growing liberalism on social issues.

Finally, both Southerners and non-Southerners believe that Southerners are different in a number of intangible (or at least unmeasured) ways: in manners, hospitality, pace, style, and all the other traits that *Southern Living* exists to celebrate and to promote, and which go to make up what we might call the texture of everyday life. I know of no hard evidence to document these differences, but, like our survey respondents, I believe they exist. I experience them whenever I leave the South and return.

So to the question whether the new Southern middle class is still culturally Southern, the answer must be yes, with qualifications. Like the elites of other modernizing societies, these people have lost—often they've consciously rejected—many elements of their traditional, "folk" culture, and I see no reactionary social movement, no Alabama ayatollah, coming forward to insist that they purify themselves. Although some residue of the traditional value orientation remains, these are not, in Herbert Gans's marvelous phrase, "urban villagers." Authoritarianism, familism, racism, and the rest—all are gone or going with the wind as peculiarly Southern traits among American business and professional people. Too bad, in some respects, and good riddance in others, in my view.

At the same time (again like the elites of other modernizing societies), the members of the South's new upper-middle class are intensely conscious of the place and role of their society, its economy and its culture, in the larger world. They are not Southern nationalists, not neo-secessionists, but they're likely to believe that what's good for the South is good for them, and probably vice versa.

And you can still tell where most of them are from without looking at their T-shirts. The middle classes of industrial nations have many things in common by virtue of that fact, but just as the middle classes of Sweden, Japan, South Africa, and the Soviet Union are recognizably Swedish, Japanese, South African, and Russian, so middle-class Southerners are, and apparently will remain, recognizably Southern. I have mentioned a few of the identifying characteristics. That T-shirt I keep mentioning gives some others, and I'll just reproduce it, to close. It's in the form of a dictionary entry. "Southerner," it says, "noun. A person born or living in the South; gracious, easy-going, slow-talking friendly folk devoted to front porches, oak trees, cool breezes, magnolias, peaches and fried chicken."

IV. The South Today

10. Plastic-Wrapped Crackers
Southern Culture and Social Change

In 1928, an unusually farsighted Southerner named Broadus Mitchell pondered the implications of the South's impending modernization, wondering "whether these great industrial developments [to come] will banish the personality of the South . . . or whether the old spirit will actuate the new performance. . . . Will industrialism produce the same effects here as elsewhere, or will it submit to be modified by a persistent Southern temperament?" More than a half-century later, the South has certainly seen its share of industrialization, urbanization, and all the other -*ations* that sociologists call development and most of us would optimistically call progress, but the answers to Mitchell's questions are still not clear.

When he wrote, a majority of Southerners were engaged—unprofitably, for the most part—in agriculture. Only a third lived in the South's towns and cities ("cities," with a couple of exceptions, that didn't amount to much anyway). The South's per capita income was roughly at the level we use today to distinguish between developed and less developed countries, and was substantially less than that in the rest of the United States. Since then, both the proportion and the absolute number of Southerners working on farms have declined dramatically (fewer than one in twelve does so now, only slightly more than the national figure), and the nature of Southern agriculture has changed; the size of the average Southern farm has doubled, and it has itself been very largely "industrialized." Per capita income in the South is now recognizably American and is a good deal closer to the national figure (although a gap still remains). The South has become, like the rest of the United States, an urban society. Over two-thirds of its people are now city or town folk, and a half-dozen of its cities are grand enough to have teams in the National Football League.

These changes and their correlates are obvious even to the casual visitor, and writing about them has become a staple of American journalism. With monotonous regularity, Northern journalists arrive at Southern airports, travel interstate highways to Holiday Inns, chat with a few new-style Southern politicians or academics, and report back that "the South has rejoined the Union," meaning that Yankee culture has finally prevailed, a century after Yankee arms did.

And, to be fair, the changes of the past fifty years have indeed transformed more than the physical landscape of the South. For better or for worse, Atlanta *is* the model of the "New South" (a hackneyed phrase popularized by an Atlantan a century ago). The benefits of the South's development are clearly evident—in the pay envelopes of Southern workers, in public health reports, in the statistics of magazine and newspaper circulation, in state budgets for education and welfare, in nearly all of the eight hundred or so indicators of Southern deficiency that Howard W. Odum compiled in his 1936 book, *Southern Regions of the United States.* Some of the unfortunate consequences of industrial and urban development are almost as obvious. With all this change going on, and nearly all of it tending to make the South look more like the rest of the country, how can the answers to Mitchell's questions still be in doubt?

Certainly there are good theoretical reasons for supposing that economic and demographic convergence between North and South should produce cultural convergence as well, and a good many people who write about the South simply assume that it has—or, anyway, soon will. The French sociologist Frédéric LePlay's formula, "land, work, folk," is a pithy summary of the generalization that in preindustrial societies the natural data determine how a living can be made, and how a society makes its living largely determines what kind of society it is. We are how we eat. In the South, conditions favorable to staple crop agriculture led to a plantation economy, which in turn produced a plantation society. Industrialization, however, has weakened the link between "land" and "work," and as the South's economy becomes less distinctive, so, according to this view, should its culture.

But although many of the most dramatic cultural differences between North and South have been decreasing (it could hardly be otherwise), an accumulating body of research suggests that it is easy to overestimate the extent of cultural convergence and to underestimate the autonomy of Southern culture. This research indicates that in many respects Southerners are still different from other Americans and that they are as different now as they have been at any time in the recent past. Moreover, these cultural differences cannot be explained in any obvious way by differences in demographic composition or economic circumstances. To paraphrase Irving Babbitt's observation about the Spanish, there seems to be something Southern about Southerners that causes them to behave in a Southern manner.

The disjunction between economy and demography on the one hand and culture on the other, between "work" and "folk," is apparently greater than many of us have assumed. The citizen of the New South may spend forty hours a week at a job indistinguishable from those of other Americans, but he will spend nearly twice as many waking hours in families and communities organized around sentiments and presuppositions somewhat different from those found elsewhere. (Even the hours on the job may be different, of course. Sociologists have rediscovered the primary work group so often that its importance should probably be axiomatic by now.) The educated, urban, factory-working Southerner remains a Southerner, and that datum often tells us as much about his tastes, habits, and values as any of the others.

Why haven't these "great industrial developments" banished the "personality of the South"? It is tempting to speculate. For example, might importing a mature industrial regime—wherein workers spend more hours off the job than on and other values compete with short-run efficiency in the managerial calculus—be less culturally disruptive than an indigenous industrial revolution? Possibly, but I suspect the explanation is less subtle than that. I think we may simply have over-emphasized the initial differences between South and North. After all, Southerners have been Americans, too, of a sort. Whatever the differences between the cultures of the South and North, they have been more like each other, surely, than either has been like that of Japan, say, or the Soviet Union or the Republic of South Africa. Industrialism must impose *some* constraints on culture, but the old culture of the South cannot have been so far out of the range consistent with urban, industrial society that it could not adapt to it—as the Japanese, Russian, and Boer cultures have adapted.

So the link between work and folk is not without slippage. Nor is it necessarily one-way. Not only have a variety of national cultures proved to be compatible with modernization, but some of those cultures have affected the nature of development, if not its extent. Can the same be said for Southern culture? Has development been "modified by a persistent Southern temperament," as Mitchell put it? Or has Southern culture been so American—or so effete—that our region's development is following pretty much the same course as the Northeast's?

So far, it is not at all obvious that urbanization and industrialization have taken any greatly distinctive turns in response to the South's culture. There are, here and there, scattered differences from the North: fewer really big cities and more middle-sized ones; a larger proportion of rural nonfarm families, employed in industry but living in the countryside; a residually lower degree of residential segregation by race (probably reflecting an older belief that one's help should be close at hand); a higher ratio of blue-collar to white-collar workers; poverty more prevalent in rural areas than in urban ones (the reverse of the non-Southern situation); a significantly lower proportion of workers belonging to labor unions; a somewhat different "mix" of industries; and (primarily as a result of the last two factors) lower industrial wages. But, by and large, with regard to things the Bureau of the Census and the Bureau of Labor Statistics think to measure, the cities and factories of the South look pretty much like the cities and factories of the rest of the country, and what differences exist are more easily explained by the timing of the South's development than by anything in its culture.

If there have been inconsistencies between Southern culture and the general American pattern of development, as some have argued, culture has had to make way for development. In their eagerness to find a seat for the South at the great American barbeque, Southern leaders seem by and large to have adopted the attitude of William Faulkner's character, Jason Compson—"I haven't got much pride. I can't afford it"—and by any standard, Southern development so far has been remarkably pell-mell and indiscriminate.

When my hometown in Tennessee turned up on a government list of cities with serious air pollution problems, the newspaper responded with an offended editorial titled "Golden Smudge." When some citizens of Charlotte complained about the proliferation of "topless" nightclubs in their city, a Chamber of Commerce official replied in defense that the clubs attract "an estimated 5000 people from other towns across the Carolinas and Virginia . . . every day." When I asked a Columbia banker what he wanted his city to become, he expressed his admiration for—Charlotte. (So much for South Carolina's traditional arrogance.) Charlotte, meanwhile, wants to look like Atlanta; and Atlanta, it seems, wants to look like Tokyo.

This single-minded focus on growth was understandable in the 1930s. Confronted with obvious and insistent problems of poverty, bigotry, ignorance, and disease, most of the South's political, entrepreneurial, and intellectual leadership felt that the evil of the day was sufficient thereto and that they could deal with the problems of industrial society when they had an industrial society to generate them. But now we have one. Although Southerners have not "gathered down by the mainstream of American life for baptism by total immersion," as George Tindall put it, the Southern economy has certainly been born again. As we begin to enjoy the fruits of that rebirth, is there any reason to suppose we can escape some of its unpleasant consequences? The South's development has not yet gone as far as the Northeast's, and we can still learn from their mistakes. Is there any basis for hoping we shall?

There may be. Southern culture may yet have its impact. Although the broad outlines of the New South are already established (the changes have already taken place), perhaps in the fine tuning some adjustments to a "persistent Southern temperament" may be made, some regional refinements introduced. The South may have some cultural and institutional resources that the North lacked—resources that can help it domesticate and assimilate industrialism and urbanization. In particular, two enduring aspects of Southern culture may be useful: the nature and extent of religious belief and practice, and a relatively great attachment to local communities. Both characteristics have been discussed by many students of the South; here I want simply to summarize some of the findings of my own research and to consider what the persistence of these traits implies for the future of the South.

In this century at least, one of the most striking differences between the South and the rest of the United States has been the nature of the South's religious life. It is no accident that the first Southern president in over a century was a Baptist Sunday-school teacher. The South, as Flannery O'Connor observed, is "Christ-haunted," and to understand the region it is necessary to understand the role religion plays in its life.

Public opinion polls reveal that nearly 90 percent of all white Southerners identify themselves as Protestant, and nearly four out of every five of these are Baptist, Methodist, or Presbyterian. (The homogeneity of Southern blacks is even greater.) The fact that the region is uniformly *anything*, that it has never had to adjust to the presence of competing religious groups, may account in part for the prominent part religion plays in the public life of the South. (The fact that it is, to a great extent, Low Church Protestant almost certainly has some implications for the nature of religion's role, but that is another, and a complicated, question.)

Poll data also indicate that regardless of their denomination Southern Protestants are more orthodox in their beliefs than non-Southern Protestants. Despite the fact that Southern Protestants believe pretty much the same thing, however, there are a number of indications that they take denominational differences more seriously.

Religious institutions play an important role in the social and spiritual life of the South. Southern Protestants are nearly twice as likely as non-Southern Protestants to assert that churchgoing is an essential part of the Christian life, and on any given Sunday they are, in fact, more likely to be found in church. They are less likely than Protestants elsewhere to feel that religion is irrelevant to the modern world, and they are more likely to feel that their churches are satisfactory as they are.

The picture of the South that emerges from these data is one of a society that takes religion seriously. Most Southerners agree on the fundamentals of religion, which allows them the luxury of disagreement on relatively minor points of faith and practice. They are satisfied with their churches, and they support them accordingly with their time and money.

It can be shown that regional differences in these matters have not become smaller in the recent past, and that there is no reason to expect that they will in the near future. Data on trends often show *change*, in the South and elsewhere, but the *differences* between South and non-South are no smaller now than a generation ago, despite the dramatic changes in Southern society since then. When statistical controls for education, occupation, and urban or rural residence are applied (to ensure that the regional differences are not due to differences in these factors), nearly all of the differences remain, and a few become even greater. Some regional differences in attitudes more or less related to religion—anti-Semitism, anti-Catholicism, opposition to the sale of alcoholic beverages, and the like—may be decreasing, but the data strongly suggest that the religion of the New South will be as vigorous and distinctive as that of the Old.

This prediction is strengthened by a look at patterns of churchgoing within the South. In general, Southern Protestants are more likely than non-Southern ones to report that they went to church on any given Sunday. But this difference is smallest for the uneducated farm population, a group that is shrinking rapidly in the South. Many of these people are moving into blue-collar occupations in Southern cities, a migration that leads almost everywhere else in the world to a decrease in churchgoing. Outside the South, urban blue-collar workers are among the people least likely to be reached by the churches, but in the South this group is as likely to go to church as its country cousins. Evidently, rural-to-urban migrants in the South take their church with them (and the polity of the Baptist church and similar groups makes it easy for them to do so).

At the top of the status ladder is another interesting difference between the South and the rest of the United States. Outside the South, educated, urban, business and professional people are less likely to be churchgoers than their white-collar employees. In the cities of the South, however, that pattern is reversed: educated business and professional people make up one of the most churchgoing groups in the region. On an average Sunday, more than half are—or at least say they are—in church, a remarkable performance for Protestants, by any standard. Whether these people set the standard for society, as one theory of leadership would have it, or are merely excellent at doing what is expected, it is significant that belonging to a church and actually attending its services are still taken-for-granted parts of upper-middle-class life in the South.

A few years ago, I wrote: "The prophet Amos foretold a day when many should 'wander from sea to sea, and from the north even to the east,' seeking the word of the Lord, in vain. In these latter days, the wayfaring stranger would be well-advised to forsake the secular North, abjure the mysterious East, and check out the South. He will find gas station signs like the one in my town, advertising on one side REGULAR 29.9, and on the other, WHEN YOU HAVE SINNED READ PSALM 51." This invitation to save and to be saved still stands. OPEC has brought about some drastic changes on one side of the sign, but the other remains—just recently, as it happens, repainted.

Another persisting aspect of Southern culture that may have some bearing on how the region adjusts to development is what has been called localism—roughly, a tendency to see communities as different from each other and to prefer one's own. There is more to this, I think, than mere parochialism. The trait seems to be related to the sense of place remarked by so many observers of Southern life and culture, a sensitivity to the things that make one's community unique and, in particular, the existence of a web of friendship and, often, kinship that would be impossible to reproduce elsewhere.

Once again, we can find outcroppings of this characteristic scattered here and there in American public opinion poll data. For instance, when asked what man "that you have heard or read about, living anywhere in the world today" they most admire, Southerners are twice as likely as non-Southern Americans to name a relative or some local notable. (Nearly a quarter do so, despite the polling organization's obvious attempt to discourage such responses.) When asked where they would live if they could live anywhere they wanted, Southerners are more likely—and have been since the question was first asked in 1939—to say "right here." When asked to name the "best American state," Southerners name their own; almost 90 percent of North Carolinians do so, for an extreme example, compared to less than half the residents of Massachusetts. Asked where they would like a son to go to college, if expenses were no problem, only New Englanders are more likely than Southerners to name a school in their own region. (Two-thirds of the Southerners did so the last time the question was asked, despite the poor national reputation of Southern schools; only 3 percent of non-Southerners chose Southern schools.)

Once again, neither trend data nor statistical controls for the economic and demographic differences between North and South give any reason to suppose that regional differences in localism are decreasing. Although prediction is always a risky business, it may be, in fact, that as conditions in the South become "objectively" more attractive, Southerners' affection for their region and their communities will become even greater.

Within the Southern population, the degree of localism is lowest among urban groups. Whether this is a genuine effect of urban life or simply reflects the fact that a great many Southern urban folk are recent migrants to their cities remains to be seen, but, even so, the people of Southern cities are more localistic, by these measures, than their counterparts in Northern cities.

How might Southerners' religion and their localism help them adjust to the momentous changes their region is undergoing? Obviously, both are useful to individuals undergoing the sometimes wrenching dislocations in their lives that go to make up what we call social change. Now more than ever, perhaps, Southerners need the assurance of personal worth and importance their religion provides; and their taste for rootedness, their sense of community, may help them cope with the disintegrative effects of mass society. (Indeed, the psychic utility of Southern culture may have something to do with its persistence.)

But social change threatens more in the South than the mental health of individuals. When pollsters asked a sample of North Carolinians what they liked best about the South, two-thirds mentioned something about the physical environment. The South, it seems, is still a pleasant place to live. But many of the region's amenities, natural and man-made, are menaced by indiscriminate development. If the towns and cities of the South are not to become examples of Southern efficiency and Northern charm (to borrow John Kennedy's characterization of Washington, D.C.), Southerners must have both the will and the ability to make them something else. It is not obvious that they have either, but they may, and if they do I suspect that localism will provide the impetus and Southern churches at least some of the means.

Of course, localism is sometimes expressed as boosterism of the crassest sort, but it needn't be. Although several generations of Southerners have, for good reason, been mesmerized by the prospect of growth and development, there are signs now of an emerging skepticism. In a recent poll, a third of a sample of North Carolinians agreed that "much of what is good about the South will disappear if the South gets as much industry as the Northeast" (and another 22 percent were undecided); and 42 percent agreed that "material progress in the South will not be worth it if it means giving up our Southern way of life" (20 percent were undecided). Many Southerners, it seems, feel they have seen the future in the cities of the Northeast, and they're not sure it works. *Their* localism may find expression in a determination to control growth and to preserve the things they value in their communities.

If this happens, we should not be surprised to find the churches of the South involved. Southern churches, black and white, have always responded to a consensus of their members, providing them with everything from leadership in the struggle for civil rights to swimming pools and segregated private schools. In practice, most of the South's churches have been splendidly democratic institutions; in consequence, when they have become politically engaged they have often done so in ways that strike outsiders as strange, or even downright un-Christian. But, as the ongoing conflict in many states over the sale of liquor demonstrates, the churches have impressive reserves of energy, money, and political power. Although these assets may often have been misdirected and dissipated in the past, I think the South is fortunate indeed to have such mighty institutions dedicated to what is seen as community well-being, and to have a tradition of voluntary and relatively selfless support for those institutions. If Southerners' views of community well-being change, we can expect the concerns and activities of their churches to change accordingly.

This essay began with some questions one Southerner was asking fifty years ago. At about the same time, another Southerner, John Crowe Ransom, advised the South to "accept industrialism, but with a very bad grace, and . . . maintain a good deal of her traditional philosophy." We can see now that Ransom's implied dichotomy was probably a false one. The South has accepted—indeed, sought—industrialism wholeheartedly, but at least some of her "traditional philosophy" remains. And these aspects of the region's culture may yet modify and meliorate the development of the South.

11. Below the Smith and Wesson Line
Southern Violence

Lately, in the South, we've seen a lot of a human type that used to be more identified with the Midwest, namely, the civic booster. My town certainly has its share, but the greatest concentration south of the Potomac and east of the Mississippi has to be found in Atlanta, "the World's Next Great City." One way Atlanta has led the nation, though, its Chamber of Commerce doesn't mention much. The 1972 edition of the Federal Bureau of Investigation's Uniform Crime Reports showed Atlanta to be number one in homicides per 100,000 population.[1]

Every year, it competes for this distinction with a number of other Southern towns. In 1972, the runner-up was Gainesville, Florida, followed by Greenville, South Carolina; Little Rock, Arkansas; Columbus, Georgia; Tuscaloosa, Alabama; Richmond, Virginia; and Savannah, Georgia. We don't find a non-Southern contender until we get to New York City, in ninth place. Think of that—the *locus classicus* of crime in the streets, three places behind Tuscaloosa! After New York, it's back to Dixie—to Raleigh, Memphis, and Lubbock. Las Vegas slips into this catalog at unlucky number thirteen, but it's followed by five Southern towns and that half-breed, Baltimore. Detroit is the only other unambiguously Northern city to make the top twenty-five, tied with Houston for number twenty.

Perhaps these data come as no surprise to you. Most people who have looked into the matter at all are aware that Southern homicide and assault rates are the highest in the nation. In the global context,

---

1. Since writing this, I have acquired the 1975 edition, showing 1975 to be a quiet year in Atlanta; it slipped to a tie for twenty-sixth place with Nashville. But 18 of the 25 Standard Metropolitan Statistical Areas with the highest rates of murder and non-negligent manslaughter were still Southern.

the American South is about as violent as South America, and New England looks pretty much like Old England.[2] But whenever I speak of these data to undergraduates, there are always some who respond with shocked disbelief. They argue—correctly, as the polls show—that Southerners aren't afraid to walk the streets. Surely it is New York, Chicago, or Los Angeles that is lawless and violent. Anyone who reads *Time* magazine knows that. Gainesville? Tuscaloosa? Charlotte? Kojak couldn't even find them on the map.

These students have not been led entirely astray by their prejudices. To state these statistics flatly, without qualification, does suggest a misleading image of Southern life. To say that there is more violence in the South is not to say that there is more *lawlessness*, except perhaps in the purely legal sense of that word.

Consider: there is more than one way a society might come to have a high level of violence. One explanation, which used to be more popular than it is now, is that some peoples just have stronger "animalistic impulses" than others. I've reached the point at which I find that almost flattering, but, still, let's reject that one, and think about two competing sociological explanations.

On one hand, we may have inefficient mechanisms of social control; people may not understand what is expected of them, or the system of sanctions that keeps most of us in line most of the time may be too weak to do the job. A situation like this produces what we mean by lawlessness; violence is *supposed* to be restrained but isn't, because the forces for order are too weak. Some of the explanations for lynching that used to be put forward were in these terms. Lynchers were said to be uncivilized (that is, not adequately instructed in what society expected of them); or, people argued, in a sparsely settled region before the advent of highly mobile police forces, it was simply impossible to keep the lid on this sort of violence.

But the fact is that some lynchings were carried out by solid, middle-class citizens who surely knew what society expected of them, and many sheriffs and other peace officers didn't *want* to prevent lynchings

2. Like most of the economically developed nations of western Europe, Britain has an annual homicide rate of around 1 per 100,000 population. Latin American statistics are sometimes unreliable, but their rates tend to range from 5 or so per 100,000 to around 20 per 100,000. Compare New Hampshire's 1972 rate of 1.7 per 100,000 (the same as Vermont's) and Alabama's 14.1 or North Carolina's 12.8.

(leave aside the question of whether they could). This suggests another way a society can have a high level of violence: it can permit or even demand violence in some circumstances. It can have, in other words, what some sociologists have called a "culture of violence."

Now, nearly all societies permit violence in some situations (in war, for example, or in self-defense). But some societies permit it in more circumstances than others; some expect or even require it in situations where others merely allow it. The "culture of violence" tag is usually pinned on groups that require or allow more violence, in more situations, than the majority culture feels is appropriate—groups like delinquent gangs, the Mafia, or the Hell's Angels. But this is clearly a difference of degree, not of kind, and there is no reason the idea will not apply as well to a regional culture as to a criminal or neighborhood subculture.

I want to argue that, in this limited sense, and in the American context, the South displays a culture of violence, that regional differences in homicide and assault owe more to regional cultural differences than to differences in the effectiveness of socialization or other mechanisms of social control. These other differences may have existed in the past. In fact, the violent strain in Southern culture, like other cultures of violence, may have originated as an adaptation to a period of anarchy. It may have begun as a frontier trait, either on the original frontier or "the frontier the Yankee made" (as W. J. Cash called the Reconstruction period). I doubt it, but a competent historian could persuade me. Even so, the origins of the trait cannot explain its persistence. I believe that some peculiar attitudes toward violence have been integrated into our region's culture and achieved a substantial measure of autonomy; they are not merely a response to rural conditions, ineffective law enforcement, or deprivation, past or present.[3]

When I say that, in the American context, the South displays a culture of violence, I mean it in the same sense that I might say, in the

3. I believe, in other words, that Raymond Gastil and Sheldon Hackney are correct. See their articles "Homicide and a Regional Culture of Violence," in *American Sociological Review*, and "Southern Violence," in *American Historical Review*, respectively. Both examine differences in homicide rates between Southern and non-Southern states, controlling statistically for other characteristics of those states, and come to the same conclusion. Although their work has been criticized on methodological grounds, their argument does not rest entirely on the statistical presentation.

Italian context, Sicily has such a culture. If we no longer have the formal apparatus of the duel, the vendetta, and the blood feud, we still have attenuated forms of institutions like these. People understand this. Sometimes the understanding has even been written into law. In the eighteenth century, for example, colonial Louisiana had a law stipulating that a woman and her lover, taken in adultery, were to be turned over to the aggrieved husband for punishment. He could do as he saw fit, but if he killed one, he had to kill both. We don't have to go back that far for these laws. Until just recently Texas had a written version of the so-called unwritten law allowing a husband to kill his wife's lover. My own state of North Carolina still has a law protecting the rights of individuals to assault others; it forbids local school board interference with the right of teachers to use corporal punishment. I think a study of Southern state laws would turn up plenty of other examples. Certainly the way juries implement these laws reflects a regional propensity not to prejudge violence, and a study of "justifiable homicide" verdicts could tell us a lot about just what it is that justifies homicide in the South.[4]

Let us examine four implications of accepting a cultural, rather than a social-control, theory of Southern violence; then I'll offer a word or two in defense of Southern attitudes on the subject (relying on the reader to frame the case—obvious enough, I should think—against them). The first implication of a cultural explanation is that many Southerners will take a lot of violence for granted, maybe not even notice it, not simply because it is so frequent, but because it is a *type*

---

4. The Texas law, as I recall, required that the adulterous couple be apprehended *flagrante delicto* and the killing be done promptly, the assumption being that if those conditions were met, the aggrieved husband could be presumed to be acting under an "irresistible impulse." Texas, of course, is not the only place where those impulses are understood, and juries elsewhere have often been inclined to acquit in similar circumstances. If the jury fails, sometimes other actors in the system can be relied on. A North Carolina judge not long ago suspended the sentence of an apparently upright young woman who murdered her apparently worthless husband at the house of his mistress; about the same time, a North Carolina sheriff neglected to gather enough evidence to indict a filling station operator who shot and killed a thief. In the latter case, the victim was a college student returning from Florida to the Northeast who drove off from a self-service gasoline pump without paying, so the case attracted more attention in the press than the killing of a garden-variety burglar; but some North Carolinians did not see the distinction.

of violence that they find "natural." A second implication is that Southerners will not be more violent than other Americans in *all* circumstances, but only in those where the culture permits or demands a violent response. A third implication is that, like other aspects of culture,
an understanding of violence and the conditions that call for it will be
learned in childhood, and that violence will emanate from the well-
socialized, not just from marginal folk who don't know or care what is
expected of them. Finally, if violence is not just an uncontrolled growth
on the surface of Southern life but is part of its cultural bedrock, we
should expect to find outcroppings of it, so to speak, in other areas of
our common life. Violence is not just something to be used when someone wants something, but something to be sung about, joked about,
played with.

The first of those implications takes us back to my unbelieving
undergraduates. It helps to explain how someone can live in a region
with a homicide rate twice as high as anyone else's and an assault rate
half again as high, and believe that the rest of the country is more
violent. I suggest that many Southerners simply do not notice what is
perfectly obvious to other Americans (and to deracinated Southerners
like sociology professors). They actually do not *see* much of the violence around them, do not register it as lawlessness, because *it is not
lawless*. It is lawful violence, in the sociological if not the legal sense:
more or less predictable, more or less expected, and (in consequence)
more or less taken for granted. It is effectively invisible—something
like wallpaper. What people notice, for more than the time it takes to
read about it, is violence that scares them, violence that is out of control, violence that could strike them regardless of what they do themselves. And that kind of violence is no more common (probably even
less common) in the South than elsewhere.

I said that a cultural explanation of violence implies that Southerners should be more violent than other Americans only in certain circumstances, defined by the culture. If it were a question merely of the
absence or breakdown of the system of social control, then we would
expect Southerners to be more violent across the board, but they are
not. The FBI indexes two other violent crimes besides homicide and
assault: robbery and forcible rape. For both of these crimes, the Southern rate is *below* the national average, strikingly so in the case of rob-

bery. If, as I've been arguing, we understand and even sometimes excuse violence in some circumstances, evidently those circumstances don't include robbery or rape.

We can get some more mileage out of those FBI statistics. The bureau lists homicides under seven headings: spouse killing spouse, parent killing child, other intrafamily homicides, one they call (rather quaintly, I think) "romantic triangles and lovers' quarrels," a category for "other arguments," and two for "felony-type" homicides, known or suspected. These last two categories the bureau defines as "those killings resulting from robbery, sex motive, gangland slaying, and other felonious activities," in other words, most of what is meant by crime in the streets. For four of the seven categories, the Southern rate is higher—about twice as high as that for the rest of the country. Arguments and lovers' quarrels and family disputes are a dangerous business in the South. But in three of the categories, the Southern rate is about the same as that elsewhere. Southern parents are no more likely than other parents to kill their children, and Southerners are no more likely to die in a felony-type murder—no more likely, that is, to experience the impersonal, professional violence of the armed robber, or the erratic, random violence of the psychopath.

The homicides in which the South seems to specialize are those in which someone is being killed by someone he (or often she) knows, for reasons both killer and victim understand. If an injustice is being committed, it's injustice of a sort that occasions less comment and produces less fear than the injustice suffered by the unsuspecting, innocent, and wholly undeserving victim of robber or psychopath. The statistics show that the Southerner who can avoid arguments and adultery is as safe as any other American, and probably safer. Although the nine most murderous states in 1972 were all Southern, if we make a rough calculation to remove the killings that grow out of family disputes, love affairs, and arguments—leaving, for the most part, what we think of as crime in the streets—then only two of the first nine states were Southern.[5]

5. This approximation was developed by applying the percentage of all homicides that were felony-type for each region to the homicide rate for each state in the region, since the bureau does not give a breakdown of felony-type homicides by state. It is

How do Southerners learn that violence is acceptable in some circumstances but not others? This aspect of culture, I suggest, is simply taken in like others. Like the words to "Blessed Assurance," the technique of the yo-yo, or the conviction that okra is edible, it is absorbed, pretty much without reflection, in childhood. Southerners learn as they grow up that some disputes are supposed to be settled privately, violently sometimes, without calling in "the authorities." Certainly Southern boys of my generation learned that; after-school fights, arranged with considerable formality, were almost an everyday occurrence. Only the absence of the possibility of death distinguished them from duels. If you were called out for some offense, you fought. I guess you could have appealed to the teacher, but that just—wasn't done. And that phrase speaks volumes. Robert Penn Warren said of his childhood in a small Kentucky town not far from the Tennessee border: "There was a world of violence that I grew up in. You accepted violence as a component of life. . . . You heard about violence and you saw terrible fights. . . . There was some threat of being trapped into this whether you wanted to or not." Just so. Culture is like that.

There are countless anecdotes to illustrate the point that this shared understanding is not just a schoolboy phenomenon. Hodding Carter, the Mississippi newspaperman, told in *Southern Legacy* of the only time he was ever called for jury duty. He was the youngest juryman and took his duties very seriously. Perhaps for that reason he was elected foreman. The case before the jury involved an irascible gentleman who lived next door to a filling station. For several months he had been the butt of various jokes played by the attendants and the miscellaneous loafers who hung around the station, despite his warnings and his notorious short temper. One morning, he emptied both barrels of his shotgun at his tormentors, killing one, maiming another permanently, and wounding a third. It was clear that the man had done it, and in the jury room Carter looked over his fellow jurors and said, "Well, gentlemen, there's no disagreement over what the verdict should be, is there?" Everybody allowed as how there was no question about it. "Well, then he's guilty." Whoa, now—wait a minute. When the

obviously crude, but may serve to give an idea of how the rankings would change if we were able to look at a more refined breakdown.

jury was polled by the incredulous judge, Carter was the only juror who recorded his vote as guilty. As one of the others put it, "He wouldn't of been much of a man if he hadn't shot them fellows." Carter, for his trouble, got a reputation as a "hanging juror" and was never called for jury duty again.

Here's another Hodding Carter story. One time he wrote an editorial one of his readers took exception to, and the man called Carter up to say he was going to kill him. (One of the rules of the game is that a warning ought to be given.) Carter, sensible man, thought about calling the police or leaving town, but he knew that if he did that, he could forget about being a newspaperman in Mississippi. "He wouldn't of been much of a man" if he'd done that. So he cleaned his gun and waited for his caller (who, incidentally, never showed up).

Compare those stories from the Mississippi Delta to H. C. Brearley's observation, made at about the same time, in the Southern mountains. "It has been found impossible to convict men of murder . . . provided the jury is convinced that the assailant's honor was aggrieved and that he gave his adversary notice of his intention to assail him."

These examples come from real life. Dozens, probably hundreds, more can be found in Southern literature. Let me just mention an unusual episode in which a literary hero *refuses* to follow the prescriptions of his culture. In Faulkner's *The Unvanquished*, after young Bayard Sartoris' father is gunned down, unarmed, by his former business partner, Bayard is expected to avenge his father's death, but will not. Instead, he confronts the murderer, unarmed, and orders him to leave town, which the man does. Bayard then undertakes, symbolically, to restore order to his disordered society—by going away to law school. I mean no disrespect for the legal profession, but I must confess that on first reading that struck me as anticlimactic, not to say unmanly. (I have since been persuaded that I did both Faulkner and Bayard Sartoris an injustice.)

Notice what is going on here. If Southern violence were due simply to a lack of social control, we would expect the most violence from those who are the least well socialized, those who have not learned to want to do what they are supposed to do. A cultural explanation means the opposite: the best socialized, those who understand what is expected of them, will be violent sometimes, because sometimes violence is what is expected. That's why Carter oiled his gun. That's why I was

disappointed in Bayard Sartoris. Sometimes people are violent because they want to be and there is nothing to stop them. But sometimes
people are violent, even when they *don't* want to be, because there
will be penalties (disgrace is a very effective one) for *not* being violent.

Finally, if violence is an integral part of our regional culture, we
ought to find it turning up in odd places here and there—in our literature, for example, and in our music, our humor, our everyday pastimes. I will leave the discussion of literature to scholars more qualified
than I am, but I will note that two of the most widely viewed television
programs of all times were adaptations of books about the South, *Gone
With the Wind* and *Roots*, and both were served up with healthy dol-
lops of violence.[6] If nothing else, this ensures that other Americans'
stereotypes of the South will continue to include violence, reinforced
by other films and cultural products as diverse as *The Heat of the
Night*, *Mandingo*, *Easy Rider*, *Deliverance*, and the entire oeuvre of
Tennessee Williams.

Of course, there is another possible explanation for the presence of
violence in these works. It could be that, since they are produced for a
national audience, the violence is just thrown in to gratify the con-
sumers' desire to believe strange things about the South. Faulkner
wrote of Northerners' "gullibility: a volitionless, almost helpless capacity and
eagerness to believe anything about the South," and Billy Carter said once
that "the Yankee press will believe any damn thing you say, and print it."
I think these gentlemen have a point, and it probably disqualifies as
evidence most works about the South produced for national consump-
tion. But violence plays a remarkable role in indigenous Southern
popular culture as well, in products and pastimes enjoyed by Southerners themselves. Through these media, violence is an ever-present, obvious, but taken-for-granted feature of our everyday lives, not just
something that surfaces on Saturday nights when the moon is full and
the corn liquor flowing freely.

Sometimes violence is celebrated in our popular culture, but it is
probably even more significant that so often it is treated as simply
natural—part of the landscape. The sheer ordinariness of violence
may indicate its importance in our lives, and our popular culture may

6. An even more widely viewed program was the episode of "Dallas" that answered the
   question of who shot J. R. Ewing. I rest my case.

both reflect and reinforce Southerners' distinctive attitudes toward violence and the use of force. By way of example, let's examine—briefly, unsystematically, and in no particular order—country music, Southern humor, and football.

Obviously, it is no longer possible to draw a hard and fast distinction between country music and popular music. Each has influenced the other, and country music has followed its audiences in their migrations, to Bakersfield, Chicago, Detroit, and throughout the country.[7] Still the music retains its identification with the South; dozens of nostalgic songs attest to that. Nearly all country-music singers are either Southern-born or only a generation removed from the South. Since the economic and demographic changes of the last few decades have affected the country-music audience, like other Southerners, and country music, so called, is now the music of an urban, blue-collar population, I am convinced that a study of country music and a comparison with other American popular music could tell us a great deal about the emerging culture of the New South, that urban, industrialized society we suddenly find all around us.

If you look for urbanization and industrialization to erode Southern attitudes toward violence, you cannot take much comfort from the statistics, which show that Southern cities are more violent than rural areas. Rural Southerners gone to town take violence with them, and this is perfectly evident in the music they listen to. I haven't done a systematic analysis of it, but if you don't believe me, just listen for a few hours to any country-music radio station. "Coward of the County," with its punch line (so to speak) "Sometimes you have to fight when you're a man," is a classic of its genre, but you'll also hear songs like "Ruby," in which a paraplegic war veteran tells his wife that he'd kill her, if he could move, for "taking her love to town." Merle Haggard is a fine singer who has based his career largely on articulating working-class *ressentiment*. You'll hear him sing "Walkin' on the Fightin' Side of Me," a song addressed to war protesters. (I haven't seen any protesters for years, but I hear the song at least once a month.)

---

7. It may be of interest that, in 1975, Bakersfield ("The Nashville of the West"—*i.e.*, the West Coast center of the country-music industry) was in the "top forty" of SMSA's with regard to its homicide rate, which was about the same as those of Mobile, Jackson, San Antonio, and Augusta.

The image of barely concealed menace that Johnny Cash exploited, before middle age and religious conversion mellowed him, is still a highly marketable commodity, as a half-dozen imitators are proving today. Cash's use of violence in his songs is perhaps most obvious in some albums recorded before audiences of prison inmates (who cheer lustily at the appropriate places). A couple of Cash's songs bear close analysis. A number called "Kate" supports Sheldon Hackney's suggestion that Southern violence is part of a cultural pattern of "extrapunitiveness"—a tendency to fix the blame for individual or societal frustration and failure on outside agencies rather than internal shortcomings (the fault is not in ourselves, but in our stars, our spouses, our parents, "society," Wall Street, or whatever). "Kate" is sung by a man in prison for murdering his wife. He sings to her:

> There's no two ways to figger
> Your cheatin' pulled the trigger.
> As sure as your name's Kate
> You put me here.[8]

Another Cash song, a very popular one, shows how country music uses violence almost incidentally, just as one of the givens of life, and how the music can often be even cheerful about violence. (Incidentally, I heard a song once with a title something like "The Old-Time, Traditional Saturday-Night, Redneck Drunken Brawl," but I never heard it again, and I am restricting my examples to songs that have achieved popular acceptance.) In "A Boy Named Sue" the protagonist at long last meets the father who gave him that name. Father and son have a good fight, "Kicking and a-gouging in the mud and the blood and the beer." Afterwards, the father explains that he named the boy Sue so that he would learn how to take care of himself, and says he is pleased to see that the plan worked.

Contrast both the prevalence and the treatment of violence in country music with that in American popular music generally. I have really only mentioned a half-dozen country songs, but I'll bet there is more violence or threat of it in those songs than in all of the "top forty" songs of the past twenty years put together. Moreover, as I have indicated,

---

8. Hackney relates this hypothetical tendency ingeniously to regional variation not only in homicide rates, but in suicide rates as well. (The two tend to vary inversely.)

country music treats violence as something ordinary and natural. On the very few occasions I can think of when violence appeared in top forty music—during the marketing of revolution in the late sixties in such songs as "Street Fighting Man" by the Rolling Stones, and more recently in punk rock—the violence is there for its shock value, serving somewhat as the pornography of the sexually liberated. Violence has no shock value in country music; it is too common, too everyday.

And certainly popular music doesn't *joke* about violence, ever. Country music sometimes does. A marvelous example is "Colorado Kool-Aid," by Johnny Paycheck. It simply defies summary, but it has to do with the comical loss of an ear in a knife fight. Southern humor in general relies heavily on violence. I am tempted to say that this is because Southern violence is sometimes so *funny*. Ever since the pre–Civil War days when Southwestern humorists made their reputations and their livings by telling funny stories about their violent neighbors, Southerners have dined out (especially when their dinner companions are Yankees) on hilarious, if hair-raising, tales of violence, many of which are even true. My own favorite is the story about the time the good people of my hometown in Tennessee hanged an elephant for murder. That happened in 1916, but there is a constant supply of new stories. In one week, while working on this essay, I heard about both a woman in Tennessee who shot her son for blowing up the Thanksgiving turkey with a cherry bomb, as his father was about to carve it, and a South Carolina man who pulled a .22 pistol and wounded a restaurateur and his wife for serving him a chicken neck in his sandwich. I could go on, but the point is that Southern humorists, amateur and professional, have a lot of raw material to work with.

Notice, however, what *kind* of violence strikes us—some of us at least—as funny. There is nothing funny about Charles Manson or Richard Speck; cold-blooded killers are not amusing. I think the common element in the funny stories is an exaggerated response to a legitimate (if somewhat grotesque) grievance, by someone we can identify with. We can share the exasperation of a mother with a malicious son, the annoyance of a customer who gets a chicken neck sandwich, even the righteous anger and fear of a group of citizens with a murderous elephant on their hands. In some sense, in each of these cases, the victim "asked for it," although I hope most of us would restrain ourselves. We cannot share the feelings of a Manson or a Speck. Their murders are in the FBI's "felony-type" category, and most of us can't understand them, much less be amused by them; they frighten us. But violence *for cause*—well, it probably ought to be punished, but it is something we can live with. It is something we *do* live with.

We also live with violence for sport. Although the taste for violent entertainment is not uniquely Southern by any means, Johnny Cash's songs, the research of some historians, and many studies of Americans' leisure-time activities suggest that Southerners enjoy both watching and participating in blood sports and other violent pastimes more than other Americans. Ponder the datum that Southern city folk are more likely to hunt for sport than non-Southern rural people. Consider the recent renaissance of organized dog-fighting, centered in the South, especially in the Southwest. Reflect on the role of football in Southern life.[9]

I know perfectly well that football is becoming (if it is not already) the great *American* pastime, but I view that as simply one instance of what has been called "the Southernization of America," and I want to argue that the game still has a place in our regional life that is unparalleled elsewhere. Where else would a house-and-garden magazine like *Southern Living* name an all-star team and publish recipes for tailgate parties? Where else would a minister conclude the invocation at a high-school game (as one did in Pflugerville, Texas) by saying "Lord, we need this one tonight. We've just got to have it"? Where else, for that matter, would a high-school football game have an invocation? Not long ago, the highest-paid state official in South Carolina was a football coach. Are there other states where that is true? If so, I'll bet they're Southern. In 1974, the South was home to only five of the twenty-six teams in the National Football League, but about 43 percent of the players in the NFL came from Southern colleges, and half the quarterbacks did. It seems we not only *like* football, some of us play it pretty well.

Not surprising, it seems to me, because in some ways the function of violence in football is a scaled-down version of its function in Southern life. It isn't the purpose of the game, but it is a legitimate and often desirable means to that purpose. Among football coaches, the

9. The data and quotations in the next two paragraphs are mostly from an unpublished paper by Raymond Manley Strunk, Jr.

"character-building" school of thought tends to emphasize the training in teamwork and self-sacrifice the game provides. That's what Chuck Mills, the Utah State coach, had in mind when he said that "football is a micro-form of the American adventure." But violence is part of the game, too, and every bit as necessary as teamwork. The difference between football and free-for-all, like the difference between Southern life and a state of nature, is that the ever-present violence is focused and channeled by a set of commonly accepted rules. I have not found a football coach to quote on the subject of football as an education in the constructive use of violence, but Konrad Lorenz, the student of animal behavior, has argued that "the main function of sport [in general] lies in the cathartic discharge of aggressive urge. . . . It educates man to a conscious and responsible control of his own fighting behavior. . . . More valuable still is the educational value of the restrictions imposed for fairness and chivalry which must be respected even in the face of the strongest aggression-eliciting stimuli." Football players learn the Southern lesson that violence is often useful and that it is allowed in some circumstances but not others.

Is a culture that accepts violence as a natural part of life and merely channels it and curbs its excesses more realistic, even more healthy, than one that sees violence as generally undesirable and tries to suppress it? The answer depends on your view of human nature; yours may be different from Professor Lorenz', and I will not get into that subject here.

Certainly, whether violence is culturally patterned or anarchic, it inevitably leads to tragedy for individuals and their families, and sometimes contributes to the oppression of entire populations. It has done both in the South. A nonchalance about violence—even if only in defense of honor—gives license to sadists and may (as it probably has in the South) encourage an exaggerated sensitivity to slights, real or imagined.

But it may be that some of us nowadays underrate the fair fight as a device for settling disputes. It simply is not true that "fighting doesn't settle anything"—and nobody knows that better than Southerners, who have seen it settle the questions of slavery and secession pretty thoroughly. If Southerners have been perhaps too quick to fight, it seems to me that they have usually coupled that tendency with a willingness to accept the outcome, win or lose.

And, as Samuel Johnson said once, although sins of excess may be no less sinful than sins of insufficiency, most of us find them easier to sympathize with. There can be an exaggerated distaste for violence, it seems to me, which is as unwholesome in its own way as bloodlust. The pacifist merits our respect, but the coward does not. One says fighting is immoral (a defensible position, although we may disagree); the other says fighting is scary, or nasty, and nothing is worth fighting for, anyway. Whatever Southerners' faults in the matter (and they've usually been obvious), our people, black and white, have witnessed with some consistency and often at great cost to the belief that there are enemies who cannot or should not be appeased, conflicts that cannot or should not be negotiated, affronts that should not be ignored—in short, that there *are* things worth fighting for. We may disagree about what those things are, but I think we can use the reminder that they exist.

12. Summertime and the Livin' Is Easy
Quality of Life in the South

Around 1930, H. L. Mencken and one of his cronies set out to study the "level of civilization" in each of the (at that time) forty-eight states. They put together a variety of quantitative indicators of health, wealth, literacy, governmental performance, and so on, and triumphantly announced in the *American Mercury* that "the worst American state" was Mississippi. Alabama was next, followed by the other eleven Southern states, with only New Mexico (at number forty) breaking up the otherwise solid South. The four "best" states were Massachusetts, Connecticut, New York, and (believe it or not) New Jersey, in that order.

Just recently, Ben-Chieh Liu published a study, *The Quality of Life in the United States*, which was much more sophisticated methodologically than Mencken's survey and substituted the more modish phrase "quality of life" for Mencken's "civilization." But it used basically the same sorts of indicators—measures of economic well-being and governmental services—and it came up with substantially the same results: the Southern states were all at the bottom of the scale. The "quality of life" in the South was apparently still the poorest in the country.

Of course Southerners have been familiar with criticisms like this for a long time—since the 1850s, anyway, when Hinton Helper's *Impending Crisis of the South* took much the same line. Helper was not the last Southerner to join Northern critics of his region; Mencken cited the "ingenious study" by S. H. Hobbs, Jr., *North Carolina: Economic and Social*, as inspiring his own "worst state" research. Those who have felt obliged to defend the South have usually replied to these critics with variations on the theme that man does not live by bread alone.

One of the most eloquent statements of this position came from the Vanderbilt Agrarians, who published their manifesto *I'll Take My*

Stand at just about the same time Mencken was collecting his statistics. Their philosophy can be summarized by the Southern folk maxim that success is getting what you want, but happiness is wanting what you get.

Now certainly there have been versions of the good society besides just one in which everybody is happy. Samuel Johnson could scoff at happiness as a criterion for quality of life. A bull, he said, standing in a field with lots of grass and a cow nearby probably thinks he's the happiest creature alive. But as Kenneth Terhune pointed out, in *The Quality of Life Concept* (a symposium published by the Environmental Protection Agency), nearly all recent discussions of the concept take it for granted that a society's quality of life *means* the extent to which it makes for individual happiness, or satisfaction, or what the economists mean by their special use of the word *welfare*. Mencken used the same criterion, quoting J. B. Bury approvingly. "A condition of general happiness is the issue of the earth's great business."

And certainly, as somebody said once, happiness is no laughing matter. I'll come back to some of the problems with using individual happiness as a defining measure of the quality of life, but for the moment let's accept the general consensus that it should be so, or at least that happiness is an important component of the concept.

One development in the social sciences since Mencken's time, and one with an important bearing on this question, is the elaboration and refinement of sample survey techniques and of social-psychological measurement. It is no longer true that "of happiness and despair we have no measure." We don't have to assume anymore that wealthy people are happier than poor ones, we can *show* this is so, and— equally important—we can show when and under what conditions it is not so. And when we ask the question, What is the worst American state? we can use an entirely different sort of indicator: direct, social-psychological measurement of satisfaction. When we do this, we get some interesting results.

Now, even if we restricted ourselves to the kind of things governments ordinarily collect statistics about, there are reasons to doubt the perennial conclusion that the quality of life in the South is relatively poor. We find striking differences in the South's favor, for example, in suicide rates, in rates of mental illness, in rates of alcoholism and heart disease and other stress-related health problems. Each of these differences is open to several interpretations, of course, but taken together they suggest we shouldn't jump to conclusions about the quality of Southerners' lives. There is also the matter of migration statistics. It is widely known by now, I suppose, that there has been net in-migration to the South for whites for some time; lately there has been net in-migration for blacks as well. The social and demographic characteristics of these immigrants suggest that many of them are responding to something more than just economic opportunity.

It's when we turn to the survey evidence, though, that the contradictions get really striking. In an essay called "Is North Carolina Really the 'Best' American State?" Merle Black looked at data from the Comparative State Elections Project conducted by the Institute for Research in Social Science. Samples of citizens from thirteen states, including the five Southern states of North Carolina, Alabama, Texas, Louisiana, and Florida, were asked, "All things considered, would you say that your state is the best state in which to live?" Overall, about 63 percent of the respondents felt they were currently living in the best state, but there was huge variation in this figure from one state to another. By this measure, the "best" of the thirteen states examined was—well, North Carolina, where more than 90 percent of the natives felt their state was the best. Alabama was the next best, followed by the other Southern states. Only California (fourth of the thirteen) ranked higher than any Southern state. The "worst" state, in the opinion of its residents, was Massachusetts—Mencken's "best" state!—where only about 40 percent of the sample felt that their state was the best, "all things considered." New York was also one of Mencken's "best" states, but it does just about as poorly. It looks as if my fellow Tennesseean, Brother Dave Gardner, may have been right when he said that the only reason people live in the North is that they have jobs there. (He said he'd never heard of anyone retiring to the North.)

For these thirteen states, the rank-order correlation between Mencken's index of "civilization" and Black's measure of satisfaction was a negative .76. The Northeastern states were civilized and discontent, the Southern states were happily backward, and the Midwest was, as usual, mediocre all the way around. Only California was above average in both respects, and only South Dakota below.

In my own work, with a series of Gallup Polls dating back to 1939, I've found very similar results. When Americans are asked where they would most like to live if they could live anywhere they wanted, a constant finding is that Southerners like it where they are better than any other Americans, except possibly Californians.

Isn't this odd? Why don't we Southerners realize how bad off we are? Or, for that matter, why don't Northeasterners appreciate how well off *they* are? Looking for expert opinions, I polled a small sample of my colleagues in the sociology department at the University of North Carolina. A few of them—transplanted Yankees—suggested that Southerners are too ignorant to know any better. But that just won't do. Most of the people who said this can be presumed to "know better" themselves, yet still choose to live in North Carolina. Besides, Merle Black's data show that, among North Carolinians generally, those with more education, more opportunities for travel, and so forth, are no less likely to regard North Carolina as the "best state" than anyone else. In Massachusetts, it's *true* that the people who "know better" like their state less, but that's not the case in North Carolina. As a matter of fact, *nothing* makes any difference in the generally high evaluation that North Carolinians have of their state. Black North Carolinians are as enthusiastic as white ones, rich ones as enthusiastic as poor ones (but no more so), urban folk like the state as well as rural ones. Only recent migrants (and I emphasize *recent*) have an evaluation of the state that is less than overwhelmingly favorable. It looks as if Thomas Wolfe was on to something when he wrote in his notebook, "New England is provincial and doesn't know it, the Middle West is provincial, and knows it, and is ashamed of it, but, God help us, the South is provincial, knows it, and doesn't care."

No, the paradox these data present cannot be explained by saying that Southerners don't know any better, although, of course, some don't. I think part of the contradiction is more apparent than real. What is a poor and ignorant Tarheel telling us when he says that North Carolina is the best state? Why, he's telling us that it's better to be poor and ignorant in North Carolina than in any other state. Sure, he would rather be rich, but he probably doubts that he can really improve his economic condition by leaving. If he thought that, he would probably leave.

Obviously it is better to be rich than poor; and if it's not obvious, there's plenty of evidence to prove it. It is not so obvious that it's better to live in a rich state than in a poor one. In fact, there are good reasons to suppose that living in a rich state makes rich folks feel less rich, and poor folks feel poorer. So any *given* individual may be psychologically better off in a state like North Carolina or Alabama, where the average individual is worse off.

Besides that, the kind of economics and politics that can make a state healthy, wealthy, and wise—"civilized" as Mencken would have it—can have at least short-run effects that people experience as debits in the quality of life ledger. For example, New York spends twice as much per pupil on education as North Carolina. Score one for the quality of life in New York when those pupils finish school. But North Carolina's taxes are about half of New York's, per capita. Score—how much?—for the quality of life in North Carolina right now. Workers earn half again as much in Illinois as in South Carolina. But they're on strike for an average of four to ten times as many days in a given year, often with negative consequences for *other* people's quality of life. Connecticut's homicide rate is only half of Virginia's. But many Virginians would find Connecticut's gun control laws an obnoxious interference with their personal freedom. New Jersey is more highly industrialized than Arkansas. But Arkansas's air is cleaner.

My point is not that the Southern states are preferable in each of these comparisons. (I, for one, would be glad to pay higher taxes to improve education in North Carolina: I have to teach graduates of North Carolina high schools.) I am just pointing out that a given individual can quite rationally be unwilling to trade a clear and present good thing for a distant and hypothetical benefit, which will probably accrue to someone else in any case. It is perfectly reasonable to want to be born in New York—you'll have a better statistical chance of surviving to adulthood, getting a decent education, and entering a high-paying occupation. But it may also be reasonable to want to *live* in North Carolina—your money will go further and you are likely to enjoy life more. (I think the migration statistics are telling us that people are starting to notice this.)

Anyway, if we recognize that workers in what we can call the "Menckenian" tradition are measuring one thing, and that the people who talk about "satisfaction" are measuring another, we have gone a long way toward explaining the apparent discrepancies. There are some interesting questions left, though. For instance, what is it about

the Southern states that their residents like so much? I've already suggested a few possible answers, but I want to press on—without fear
and without research, as Carl Becker said once—to argue that there
are things that almost everybody wants and that Southerners have
more of. I think we can explain why Southerners like their communities and their states so much—and it isn't that the climate affects their
brains directly (as one of my colleagues suggested).

Let me describe a whimsical quality of life index I constructed, one
I think does a fantastically good job of predicting which states are lov-
able and which aren't. This index has two components: *mean winter
temperature* and *robberies per 100,000 population* in 1971. These two
factors explain nearly two-thirds of the variation in the ranks of the
states on Merle Black's "best state" question. Obviously, people like
safe, warm places.

This finding tells us more than that, though. It's a roundabout way
of telling us what is *important* to people when they're deciding whether
some place is a good place to live. Each of those components—climate
and robberies—is standing in, so to speak, for a host of other characteristics. The average winter temperature has all sorts of implications
for people's way of life (or "life-style," if you prefer). And the robbery
rate tells us something about personal relations and social stability. I
suggest that this is the sort of thing people have in mind when they say
that North Carolina is the best state—or that Massachusetts isn't.

In 1971, Glen Elder and I asked a sample of North Carolinians,
"What would you say is the *best thing* about the South?" More than
two-thirds of our respondents mentioned natural conditions: the benign
climate, the clean air, the forests and wildlife, the easy pleasures of a
life lived largely outdoors. There's nothing uniquely Southern about
this taste: the frequent mob scenes in our nation's parks tell us that.
But Southerners can indulge themselves more easily and more often
than their less favored brethren—and our data show that that's important to them.

Incidentally, I don't think it's accidental that the climate hasn't
turned up in most quality of life indexes. Most of them have been
constructed by intensely practical folks, concerned with *policy*—and
there's not a whole lot the government can do about the weather. At
least not yet. Thank God. Dr. Johnson wrote, "How small of all that

human hearts endure,/That part that kings or laws can cause or cure"—words to make a political scientist gnash his teeth. But we need to keep them in mind when we talk about what makes people happy.

The other component in my little index, the number of robberies per 100,000 population, reflects another major concern of Americans: what was called, not too long ago, "crime in the streets." Poll after poll shows that many Americans just don't feel safe. It has been almost traditional to put the homicide rate into quality of life indexes—and the South doesn't do too well on that score. But the thing about homicide, especially in the South, is that it's not "in the streets." It's often in the home and usually between friends, and even in the South it's pretty unusual. What is more common, and what people are scared of, is being robbed, mugged, raped, or burgled by a *stranger*. And North Carolina's robbery rate is only one-tenth of New York's.

I think in some ways the most important implications of the robbery rate are indirect. Suspicion and distrust, the absence of easy and cordial interaction with strangers—this kind of thing is important to people, too. When we asked what the best thing about the South was, half of our respondents said the *people* were, that Southerners are friendly, polite, take things easy, and are easy to get along with. Two recent studies from the University of Michigan document the obvious fact that personal relations are important to *all* Americans; we all rely on face-to-face interaction for the greater part of the satisfaction we get from life. But the North Carolinians in our poll seemed to feel (and I agree with them) that the texture of day-to-day life is pleasanter in the South, particularly in fleeting, secondary interactions (like those with salesclerks and secretaries and cabdrivers and policemen). A good part of nearly everybody's day is taken up with precisely that kind of interaction. It might as well be pleasant.

Here again, the effects of government and economy are really pretty remote. The kinds of things that Mencken and other toilers in that vineyard are measuring don't have much to tell us about this aspect of quality of life. Southerners know what Mencken was trying to tell them. Very few of our respondents mentioned politics or economics when we asked them what they liked about the South, and nearly a third mentioned them when we asked what they liked least about their region. All in all, I read these data to say that state and local politics don't make much of an impression on most folks just living day-to-day, except as an entertaining sideshow (perhaps especially entertaining in the South).

If I had the time—and the weather weren't so nice—I could probably go on to explain the rest of the variation in the lovability of the states. I would start with observed facts (like that homeowning is an important value for most Americans) or with sound theoretical propositions (like that people are more comfortable in culturally homogeneous communities), and I would translate those into measures we could look up in the *City and County Data Book*. But I hope I've made my point, or rather points. Let me spell them out, to wrap this up.

First, we need to be clear whether we are talking about the quality of life of a given person or of the average person. Second, nearly all good things come at a price, and we need to be sensitive to that. Third, we cannot impose our own definition of "good things" on people; they will perversely continue to use their own. Fourth, there are many important aspects of the good life that policy makers can't do anything about. And, last, Providence has seen fit to endow the South with more than its share of this bounty. We can be thankful for that.

13. The Same Old *Stand*?

When the Southern Agrarians took their stand, they did it stoutly, on two feet. Some emphasized the *Southern*, others the *Agrarian*, but fifty years ago it seemed that the two loyalties, to the South and to rural life, could (indeed, pretty well had to) go together.

Today, though, that juxtaposition is less self-evidently sensible. If ever a society can be said to have repudiated agrarianism, the South, to all appearances, is it. Two-thirds of all Southerners now are urban, by Bureau of the Census standards; of the rural third only a fraction are employed in agriculture, and of those a good many are proprietors or hands in "agribusiness"—an expression that some of the Agrarians blessedly did not live to encounter.

It is still possible to combine an affection for the South with an appreciation of the virtues and strengths of the family farm and rural life, but someone who is not prepared to exclude most residents of the South from the category *Southerner* must recognize that it is no longer a matter of defending a Southern way of life against industrialism. Increasingly, that way of life *is* industrialism.

Many feel, of course, that neither the South nor agrarianism has much to be said for it. To hell with them. But even those who find *I'll Take My Stand* pretty much right-headed on both counts must choose, in a single essay, which leg to stand on.

Whether the Agrarians' ideas on the proper relation between work and leisure, on the importance of humanizing scale, on respect for nature, on autonomy and self-respect—whether those ideas can be translated into an urban and industrial context is an important question, and one, I believe, not yet answered. That side of the Agrarian argument may be more appealing now than it was fifty years ago. We are hearing versions of it from such unlikely quarters as the governor of California and the *Mother Earth News*, and it does seem to be better received in

Vermont and Colorado than in the South, but at least it is alive and well somewhere.

It seems to me that those arguments can pretty well take care of themselves. What needs to be reasserted is the other half of the Agrarian position, the case for provincialism—in particular, the case for the South. What is now unusual about *I'll Take My Stand* is less the "small is beautiful" motif than its unshakable affection for the South; less the insistence that the South has something to offer the rest of the country as an exemplar of an agrarian civilization than the assumption that the South has something to offer Southerners. Some of the Agrarians valued the South because they believed it embodied their social ideals; most, I suspect, cherished it because it was home.

Why do Southerners, most of us, love the South? Why should we? In these times, those questions might be rephrased as: What *good* is it? Is the South any different, anymore, from the rest of the United States? If so, what differences are likely to remain, and what good are *they*?

Let me proceed in the approved Southern manner, with a lengthy anecdote about a particular individual, which, despite appearances, does have a point. This story is set in Cambridge, Massachusetts, in the early 1960s, and concerns a young Tennesseean, an undergraduate at the Massachusetts Institute of Technology.

At that time, Cambridge was not a comfortable place to be a Southerner. To this young man, it seemed that his Southernness, which he had never thought much about, was often being thrust upon him. After a few months he began to understand that, however unimportant his origins seemed to him, they were an important datum for others, a marker that they used to orient themselves to him, at least at first. The more ill-mannered of his Northern acquaintances made it clear that they saw him as a curious specimen of some sort; a few, at least, saw his Southernness as *the* salient fact about him, overriding all others. About the seventeenth time he was held personally responsible for Little Rock and Clinton (places he'd only heard of) and for Scottsboro and Gastonia (places he hadn't heard of), the novelty began to wear off.

He found that other Southern boys were going through the same sort of thing, and they used to joke about the bottomless ignorance and boundless credulity of their New York and New England friends.

Many of these folks, whether smugly self-righteous or innocently curious, would apparently believe anything at all about the South, provided only that it was weird. (Some years later he discovered that William Faulkner had said very much the same thing.) When he ran out of true stories to entertain his Yankee friends, he was not above talking about things he knew of only at second hand—swamps and alligators, footwashing and snake handling, moonshining and stock-car racing. When he found a truly gullible listener sometimes he really laid it on. (For years he remembered with embarrassment a somewhat drunken account of darkies dancing down Main Street on Robert E. Lee's birthday.) The only excuse for him is that he was eager to please, and he had discovered that a Southerner who denied that there was anything particularly interesting about the South ran into almost palpable disappointment, if not the suspicion that he was hiding something.

Some of his friends were more aggressive. One of them, an Arkansas boy, took to telling Radcliffe girls (who invariably asked) that race relations back home were just fine, that blacks were now allowed out until ten o'clock at night, midnight on Saturday. His friends from less notorious Southern states made allowances for his exasperation.

The result of all this was that Southerners in Cambridge at that time almost *had* to think about the South. Even the most deracinated began to wonder whether the observation that they were not "typical Southerners" was the compliment it was intended to be, since the speaker's idea of the typical Southerner had little to do with the people they had grown up with.

Certainly this young man began to think. What was this Southernness he was apparently stuck with? Why was he moved to defend the South? What was it to him? People assumed that he had things in common with other Southerners, but (aside from being on the receiving end of that assumption) did he? These weren't easy questions for a nineteen-year-old. But since he had plenty of other things to think about (he was no Quentin Compson), they didn't weigh too heavily on him. Nevertheless, he did wonder about them from time to time, and they set him up for his first encounter with *I'll Take My Stand*.

Browsing at the MIT bookstore one day in 1963, he ran across the Harper paperback. The title caught his eye, and the authors, Twelve Southerners, made the book sound even more interesting. He bought it and started reading John Crowe Ransom's essay, "Reconstructed but

Unregenerate," as he walked back to his room. For a Tennessee boy at the Massachusetts Institute of Technology who was having his doubts about both Massachusetts and technology, the book was a bombshell. For someone who felt moved to defend the South, this fire-eating counterattack was a revelation. It suggested an entirely new line: not "We're as good as you," not "We're no different from you," but, by God, "We're better than you." Hot stuff, in those defensive days.

But after the first enthusiasm wore off, he started having second thoughts. What was all this about agriculture? It was clear to him, thirty years after the Agrarians, that most Southerners had nothing to do with agriculture. Surely, the point of the book wasn't that he and most of his friends weren't really Southerners after all. He liked the country people he knew, but *they* weren't typical Southerners. Moreover, he'd spent possibly the worst summer of his life working tobacco for four dollars a day. Idealizing the agricultural life would take some doing. What really appealed to him was the book's unabashed championship of the South, its forthright assertion that the South was doing something right. Now if he could just figure out what that was.

His Northern friends mostly assumed that the heart of the matter was racism. He learned later that they weren't alone in this assumption; U. B. Phillips, a distinguished historian from Georgia, had argued the same thing some decades before. Unflinching support for white supremacy, he had said, was "the central theme of Southern history and the cardinal test of a Southerner." But that just didn't *feel* right. Segregation had no charms for him, or for most of his Southern friends in Cambridge, and they resisted and resented the idea that Jim Crow was the essence of Southern life and culture.

This position on race wasn't ideological; it was based on their experience. They might have felt different if they had come, like Phillips, from the Black Belt. But they didn't. They came, mostly, from the periphery—east Tennessee, Arkansas, east Texas—or from the cities and suburbs of the "New South"—Atlanta, Winston-Salem, Baton Rouge. In those settings, for whites anyway, race was simply *not very important.* Of course, all of them knew, and a few of them were, white supremacists, but (the undergraduate reflected) race was clearly not the obsession that it should have been if it was as central to their lives as everyone assumed it was. And yet they were Southerners—as they were often reminded and soon began to insist.

There were, in addition, a couple of newfound black friends—like him, young men from the South, displaced in New England. He did not discuss his musings with them; in fact, he tended politely to avoid the subject of the South, and they did, too, probably for the same reason. But he came to realize, and to hope that they realized, that he and they had a good deal in common, at least compared to the Northerners around them. They spoke in similar accents and in a similar allusive, anecdotal way; they knew the same Baptist and Methodist hymns and had the same trick of quoting or paraphrasing Scripture in outrageous contexts; they liked the same foods (although the blacks, like most of those he came to know later, preferred Scotch whisky to bourbon, for some reason); and they seemed to share a good many assumptions that he couldn't quite put his finger on. Whatever Southernness was, he came to believe, it obviously included them—unless they chose to reject it.

So, he concluded, his Northern friends were just wrong. The South no more depended on segregation than it did on subsistence agriculture. Both had been fateful influences on the South, each had left its mark, but neither was the sine qua non of Southernness. Sometimes he was tempted, when under attack, to adopt a line from the Southern comedian, Brother Dave Gardner: "I love everything about the South. I even love *hate*." But it wasn't really necessary to defend segregation in order to defend the South. To be sure, he thought, white supremacy could be defended by thoughtful and humane people (he knew some); but that observation merely proved to his satisfaction that thoughtful and humane people could be wrong, and unintentionally wicked. Perhaps because he was very young, this conclusion struck him as both profound and depressing.

But he was no closer to learning what *did* define the South. Off and on, as his circumstances allowed, he had begun to read and, in a most un-Southern way, to theorize about it. He rejected out of hand one possibility suggested by his reading. The South no longer depended (if it ever had) on the myths and imagery of the Lost Cause. The Stars and Bars, "Dixie," the whole Confederate heritage—all were dandy to use for annoying Yankees, and all served as a kind of Masonic code for white Southern boys, especially outside the South. But these symbols did not seem genuinely to move most Southerners of his generation. The last Confederate veteran had died, in his own hometown, while he was in high school; what he remembered of the event was the amused local speculation that the old boy's war record was fictitious, invented to chisel a veteran's pension from the Commonwealth of Virginia. The United Daughters of the Confederacy soldiered on, but they were as remote from the real life of his town and as faintly ridiculous as the Daughters of the American Revolution, to whom, he realized dimly, they were somewhat inferior, as these things are reckoned. People still stood up for "Dixie" at football games, but they would give that up without protest a few years later. Some of his high school friends once ran the Stars and Bars up the school flagpole on the anniversary of Appomattox, but they'd have flown the swastika or the hammer and sickle, if they'd had one, with the same fine, thoughtless, apolitical desire to raise hell.

No, time and Yankee textbooks had eaten away the core of Confederate sentiment. The little they had left was being undermined in the early 1960s by the Southern defenders of segregation, who had pretty well appropriated the Confederacy's flag and anthem. Their considerable success in identifying their own lost cause with the earlier one was, he felt, a shame.

He recognized that—like agriculture, like white supremacy—the Civil War had helped to form the South he knew. But, he believed, it had long since ceased to play an important part in sustaining it. Once again, it seemed his conclusions were only negative.

Time passed, several years' worth. The undergraduate became a graduate and married a Southern girl. His penchant for brooding about questions of little practical consequence led him to drift more or less inevitably into graduate school, in New York City, where something he had noticed in Cambridge finally sank in.

In New York, even more than in Cambridge, it was borne in on him that, in the urban Northeast, almost everyone had what he thought of as a backup identity. Not just some of his best friends but *most* of his best friends were Jewish. Those who weren't were Italian or Irish, or Puerto Rican or Polish. Everybody was *something*, even if only WASP, a label applied to those who couldn't do any better. What was he? Didn't being Southern mean much the same thing to him, serve many of the same functions, social and psychological, as his friends' ethnic identities? Wasn't there at least an analogy there?

This wasn't a particularly original idea; other people had been saying much the same thing for years (although he was pleased with himself for figuring it out independently). Still, it seemed to offer a key to understanding many of the things that had puzzled him since his first months in Massachusetts.

For one thing, relations among Southerners in the Northeast were very much like those he observed among his Jewish friends. It wasn't so much that they *liked* each other better than they liked non-Southerners (although, other things being equal, they probably did). Rather, they knew more quickly whether they liked one another or not. Because a background of understanding and shared experience could be assumed, interaction could proceed without the preliminary, tentative sort of negotiation that characterized their initial relations with non-Southerners. Even at a later stage, there were fewer surprises, fewer misunderstandings. They understood each other's humor to be humor, for instance, and usually found it funny, which was not always the case in relations with non-Southerners. There was just a lot less explaining to do.

There was, in addition, the relation between a group's identity and its past. Clearly, his Jewish friends had no more to do with the *shtetl* than he had to do with sharecropping. The Troubles were no more an ever-present burden to his Irish friends than Reconstruction was to him. His FORGET, HELL! cigarette lighter had about the same historical significance as a KISS ME—I'M ITALIAN button. It became evident, to him at least, that ethnicity as he came to know it in New York was an American creation, and a recent one. Group identity had been forged and reinforced in interaction with other groups, and its relation to the group's actual history (as opposed to the myth of that history it created for itself) was very tenuous indeed.

But these other groups, he observed in New York, resisted the melting pot, just as the Agrarians would have had Southerners do. Various social scientists were starting to document the cultural differences that American ethnic groups maintained, in the aggregate—differences that presumably explained the greater "easiness" of relations within particular groups. Clearly, though, while a group's culture might reflect its origins in some refracted way, that culture was being sustained and employed in quite different circumstances.

Like other ethnic identities, he concluded, Southernness had two aspects: on the one hand, an undeniable core of shared meanings, understandings, and ways of doing things (particularly evident in the presence of those who do not share them); on the other, outsiders' insistence that one's group membership was significant, and their expectations based on that datum. This conclusion was somehow comforting. Locating Southernness as a special case of a more general phenomenon not only seemed to explain a lot, but it made the whole business more normal, less troublesome, and, in an odd way, more "American."

So he found at least a partial and tentative answer to one of his early questions. What was Southernness to him? It was an important answer to the question, Who are you?—a question common in a fluid and pluralistic society. And it was a label for a cultural community where he could be relatively sure of being understood—not necessarily accepted, but *understood.*

But the content, the organizing principles and the shared assumptions, of that cultural community still remained tantalizingly out of reach. He thought of Southernness, inelegantly, as something like an onion. He had, to his own satisfaction at least, peeled away the dry brown outer layers that first met the eye but that had lost their former vitality, and he was left with a solid, pungent nucleus. But while he felt he knew what made up that core, he was not much closer to being able to describe it. The observables—food, speechways, music, and the like—were signs, markers, symbols of that quiddity, but not the thing itself. Later, he was to read and listen with a sense of recognition as blacks strove to articulate the mystique of *négritude* and of "soul," and he came to realize that for Southerners, as for other ethnic communities, the essential qualities of the group may be, finally, ineffable—although to allow that possibility was far from allowing that they might be illusory or that there was no further point in trying to identify them.

It may seem that this third-person account has led us rather far from *I'll Take My Stand*, and indeed it has. The point is that Southernness is a more complicated business than it appeared to be in 1930. It's no longer a matter of taking one's stand in the lower right-hand quadrant of the United States and hurling defiance at an alien industrial civilization. For better or for worse, the South finally has "rejoined the Union" (as journalists are fond of saying). The region is increasingly and, it appears, irreversibly bound up with the rest of the country. It has become more and more difficult for Southerners to live out their lives entirely in the South, entirely with other Southerners. Unreflective, reflexive Southerners can still be found, and perhaps we can be thankful for that, but they are like the snail darter, threatened by the advance of that modern regime the Agrarians warned us about. We might wish it otherwise, it may yet be a Southern characteristic to wish it otherwise, but to believe it otherwise is to display the sort of romanticism and wishful thinking that lost us a war.

But perhaps this case history, this narrative of a young Tennesseean, can serve as an example, if not an argument *a fortiori*, suggesting that the implications of "the facts" are not straightforwardly antipathetic to the continued existence of Southern culture and identity. Like other "primordial affiliations" (in Edward Shils's phrase), other ties based on blood and soil, Southernness provides a substrate beneath the overlay of functional and utilitarian relationships imposed by a modern industrial economy. Its evidences can't be kept down; it continues to crop up here, there, and everywhere, like grass through concrete.

One particular aspect of our region's culture seems to be not only surviving under these new conditions but actually thriving. This trait has always been present in the South's cultural ecology, but (like goldenrod along new highways) it benefits from the elimination of its natural competitors by urbanization and industrial development. I am referring to our regional variant of what used to be seen as the *American* trait of individualism. This characteristic has always coexisted uneasily with some other Southern traits—particularly those that the South has shared with other folk cultures, traits that characterize all rural, village, and peasant societies (which is what the South has been, in the American context, until very recently). Such characteristics as parochialism, fatalism, authoritarianism, ethnocentrism, and categorical resistance to innovation have been Southern characteristics, in the sense that Southerners have been more likely than other Americans to display them. But the same catalog could be (has been) applied to other premodern societies, to Iran, Turkey, Sicily, Mexico, and Ireland, among others. This bundle of traits, which Harold Grasmick has called *the* traditional value orientation, is menaced everywhere by urbanization and industrialization. The Agrarians knew this. That list of deceptively Latinate, "scientific" and ostensibly nonevaluative terms includes some of the things they cherished most about the South. These characteristics are indeed linked, as effect to cause, to rural and small-town life and to agricultural pursuits. In the South, as in other modernizing societies, they survive most strikingly among the rural, the poor, and the uneducated, those who are isolated from urban life, the industrial regime, and the media of mass communication.

The same traits survive, in attenuated form, among many other Southerners. The majority of us, after all, are no more than a generation removed from the countryside. But the prognosis for these aspects of Southern distinctiveness is not favorable. In many of these respects, the South's urban and suburban middle classes are already well-nigh indistinguishable from their non-Southern counterparts; in others, a difference remains, but who can say for how long? It may be that the South will hang on to a residuum of these cultural characteristics, a souvenir of its agrarian past. But such a vestige will only provide a traditional, folkish flavor to the standard industrial entrée; it will not be the foundation for a competing civilization, not the sort of thing manifestos are made of.

Alongside the folkish, organic strain in our region's culture, however, there has always been a stubborn, individualist, "I'm as good as you" outlook, a collection of cultural themes that competed with and undermined the demands of prescription, hierarchy, and organic community. The openness of early Southern society, the possibilities for individual mobility, meant that the would-be hierarchs of the South had to resort to slavery to keep their retainers in place. The varieties of Christianity that were equipped by their histories to legitimize a prescriptive order never fared well among those folk who needed encouragement to do their duty in the station in life to which it had pleased God to call them, at least not after they had the opportunity to choose something else. Throughout the South's history, those whites who seemed intended to fill the lower ranks of Southern society showed a disturbing tendency to take off for the hills or the frontier. If they stayed around, they lingered, not as humble servitors, but to display the prickly independence of men whose God has told them they are as good as anybody else, and better than the unsaved. Many Southern blacks adopted the same stance, as soon as they were able. It is significant, for instance, that after 1865 the new freedmen widely refused to work in gangs under supervision and forced Southern landowners to turn to a sharecropping system based (in theory at least) on a contract between two autonomous parties.

These two competing visions, the individualist and the organic, can be illustrated by a series of oversimplified contrasts—Jefferson and Fitzhugh, Baptists and Anglicans, yeomen and planters, Huey Long and Harry Byrd, perhaps uplands and low country. One of the unresolved contradictions of *I'll Take My Stand*, some critics have observed, is that of which South it is defending. In fact, the combination, however unstable or philosophically unsatisfying, may have something to be said for it, if each of these tendencies served to check the excesses of the other. But that question is neither here nor there, if I am right. The erosion of the folkish South by twentieth-century economic and demographic changes has left the South's version of laissez-faire free to develop relatively unchecked by prescriptive obligations and restraints based on family position, rank, class, or even race. (Sex remains, perhaps, a different matter.)

The characteristics that I am clumping under the label *individualism* differ from the traits that Southerners have shared with those from other folk societies in at least two ways. In the first place, they seem to exist sui generis, so to speak, reflecting the unique circumstances of the South's settlement, development, and historical experience; they are by no means universal among or unique to "traditional" societies. In the second place, indicators of these traits "behave" differently when examined statistically. They differentiate educated, urban and suburban, modernized Southerners fully as much as poor, rural, and uneducated ones. Regional differences in these respects show little sign of disappearing—indeed, they often seem to be increasing.

These cultural presuppositions are easier to illustrate than to list. They are displayed with greatest clarity, perhaps, in the dominant religion of the South, a brand of Evangelical Protantism that cuts across denominational lines and, for that matter, probably characterizes the beliefs of most of the unchurched. Students of the subject agree that the South is unique religiously because it is dominated by Low Church Protestant groups, notably the Southern Baptists, but also Methodists, Presbyterians, and other denominations that tend to imitate the more successful Baptists. These groups emphasize the individual's salvation and his role in accepting it. "The Hour of Decision," as the Reverend Mr. Graham tells us, is *now*, and it is up to the individual to choose, to accept the freely offered gift of salvation. Nobody else can walk the lonesome valley, as the old song has it. You've got to walk it by yourself. Others can and do help, but ultimately you're on your own. The Catholic doctrine of the Church as the Body of Christ is, in this view, an elegant metaphor at best, a mystery (in the simplest sense of that word) at worst. The Church is seen as an inorganic aggregate of individual congregations, themselves convenient gatherings of voluntarily associated individuals, each of whom maintains his own unmediated personal relation to transcendent Deity. The South's economic life increasingly relies on a complex hierarchical and specialized division of labor, but its religious economy is what the textbooks call a Robinson Crusoe situation.

Whatever else can be said about it, there is no question that this individualistic emphasis in Southern religion is comfortably consistent with other aspects of Southern culture. Just as Southerners are expected to work out their own salvation without calling on the formal institutional apparatus of Church, priest, and Sacrament, so we have often been inclined to work out our own justice without running off to the legislature or the courts. In the South, the State has no more monopoly on the means of justice than the Church has on the means of grace. To concede all legitimate coercion to the State would be repugnant to many Southerners, if not to most. Ultimately, individuals must have the ability—indeed, may have the obligation—to settle such matters for themselves. A closer look at the South's homicide rates, perennially twice as high as the rest of the country's, bears this out. The sort of murders the South specializes in are not assaults on innocent and inoffensive citizens going about their business; they are, rather, responses to attacks on someone's person, honor, or self-esteem. They are in fact private attempts, however excessive or misguided, to redress grievances. Collective violence has followed much the same pattern.

Some historians are now emphasizing the strong "Celtic" strain in Southerners' ancestry, and it is pleasant to recall that another Celtic nation has as its motto *Nemo me impune lacessit*, or, in Southern, "Nobody messes with me and gets away with it." Although this handsome boast expresses for Southerners, as for the Scots, an ideal rather than a fact, what it threatens is clearly not a lawsuit.

A respect for individualism and self-reliance is also increasingly evident in Southerners' economic views. Let me tell another story. I asked an older man recently what had happened to a brilliant black athlete from his town, who had played outstandingly for four years at a Southern university only to have his professional career cut short by injuries. He had returned, I was told, to the middle-sized Southern city where he'd gone to college, as an executive in a predominantly white business. "He married a white girl, you know, but he's doing very well." Fifty years ago, that would have been one dead black man. No amount of athletic or commercial success would have offset his breach of racial etiquette; success, in fact, would have compounded the offense. But my informant mentioned the man's marriage as he might have alluded to some bad habit, and his tone in general was one of approval, even of pride in a local boy made good.

I don't pretend that this reaction would be universal, or even typical, but it is increasingly widespread. Particularly among the Southern middle class, we find a belief system that Fitzhugh and probably some of the Agrarians would have despised. An individual is entitled—indeed, obliged—to work out his own well-being; he is free to compete, without prescriptive restraints; and he is free to enjoy the fruits of success—even a white wife—if he succeeds. Public opinion polls have shown a substantial increase of late in the proportion of Southerners who support conservative (that is, laissez-faire) economic policies, along with an increase in those who support liberal social policies. The apparent contradiction is only in the cockeyed terms of American politics; in both respects, Southerners increasingly display a version of libertarianism, the natural political expression of an individualistic ethos long evident in other institutional spheres.

Cynics may argue that this represents merely another strategic retreat, a new and more sophisticated stance in defense of race and class privilege. If top-dog Southerners can no longer get away with holding back other groups, as groups, their new ideology assures at least that those others will not be helped, categorically, to threaten the top dogs' "hegemony." There may be something to this argument. It must deal with a great deal of "false consciousness" on the part of Southerners who are hardly top dogs; but it may be, for example, that the truly incredible rates of individual upward mobility that have accompanied the South's recent economic development are encouraging people to have aspirations that will eventually prove unrealistic.

In any case, the increasingly dominant Southern doctrine is an internally consistent one, perhaps for the first time, and it is a form of libertarianism. When middle-class Southerners tell us, as most now do, that blacks should not be held back economically by Jim Crow laws or employment discrimination, that they'd be pleased to have as a neighbor anyone who can afford to live in the neighborhood, that their neighbors' children should go to the same schools as their own—when they say all this, their sincerity is not impugned by their practical indifference to those, black and white, who fail the sink-or-swim test of a laissez-faire economy. They believe that well-being is ultimately a man's own lookout, and he ought to be able to work it out without the help of institutions like government, unions, and the like (although other individuals—kinfolk, neighbors, and Christians generally—ought to help him if he needs it and they are able). Like those who achieve salvation, those who achieve economic success are entitled to the benefits, regardless of what they were before. Those who don't succeed— well, they may get helped, but like the unsaved, they will get exhortation and Christmas baskets, and hardly as a matter of *right*.

If, as I believe, the South is refining and beginning to exemplify a world view that puts individual responsibility at the heart of things and insists that individuals should—and, by and large, do—get what they deserve, it presents some interesting, homegrown features. One of the most common theoretical objections to pure libertarianism—that it destroys community—simply does not seem to apply to the Southern variety, as it is actually put into practice in most Southern towns and institutions. Community seems at least as healthy in the South as elsewhere, and I don't think it is merely as a residue from the region's preindustrial past. Here again, we can look at Southern churches as a useful microcosm of Southern society. If we can understand their cohesiveness, perhaps we can see the same processes at work in other Southern settings.

Southerners incline to the view that churches are simply voluntary associations for the benefit, in the last analysis, of the individuals who make them up—a view so taken for granted that many Southerners cannot conceive that there is any other way to think of the Church. The proposition "Love it or leave it" seems perfectly reasonable to many Southern churchmen. From time to time, groups *do* leave, to set up their own congregations or to found entirely new denominations. This mode of response results in both homogeneity and considerable group loyalty—in the new groups obviously, but also in the old.

The same phenomenon can be observed at the community level.

Congregationalism in the churches of the South (whatever their formal polity) is echoed by localism, especially in smaller communities. Southerners' relations to their communities are not merely utilitarian; loyalty is expected and is usually forthcoming, but it is also freely chosen. The prototypical Southern sentiment may be the bumper-sticker admonition, GET YOUR HEART IN DIXIE OR GET YOUR ASS OUT, a sentiment applying, *mutatis mutandis*, to churches, communities, and even business and industrial enterprises, as well as to the region as a whole. But, paradoxically, this species of apparent intolerance is not wholly antithetical to individualism. In a way, individualism is its prerequisite, for the individual must be free to choose: salvation or damnation, right or wrong opinions, loyalty or treason, to stay or to go. "Love it or leave it" is said only to free men.

"Leaving," of course, need not be physical (although it often is). As Southerners have shown repeatedly, it is no longer necessary to go to Rhode Island or to Utah to set up a new religious denomination, and someone willing to be lonesome can usually withdraw from the life of a Southern town without heading for points west or north. But in order to be part of a community, one must adhere to community standards, or else start a new community with like-minded individuals. In theory, nonconformity can be dealt with by suppression, by abandoning group standards altogether, or by excluding the deviant from the group. It seems to me that Southerners usually prefer the last of these solutions, although the first gets more publicity.

The old joke about both of our churches worshiping God—you in your way, we in His—summarizes an anomaly that has puzzled many observers of Southern life. Theoretical hostility toward other groups, other communities, and other regions is often combined with a sort of workaday pluralism that lets folks get along pretty well most of the time, although it wouldn't satisfy the sponsors of National Brotherhood Week. Southerners quite often tolerate the theoretically intolerable from "outsiders," reasoning that what those people do is of no concern to us. An element of circularity defines outsiders, in part, as those who think or do the intolerable. Whatever else may be said about this solution, it seems to me that it's usually preferable to trying to make outsiders conform to insider standards, and always superior to concluding that there is nothing that could be called intolerable.

In return, Southerners would like a similar toleration for themselves.

"If you don't like the way I'm living," Nashville's Charlie Daniels sings, "just leave this long-haired country boy alone." The coiffure has changed, but the sentiment is as old as the hills to which Daniels' ancestors migrated in order to be left alone. And, it should be noted, today's long-haired country boy is likely to be a loyal member of a group of long-haired country boys who are tolerated by the rest of the community, as long as they keep their intolerable tastes and habits to themselves and only knife each other.

What has always particularly annoyed Southerners is not what others do among themselves but others' attempts to make us do differently. My reading of the defenders of slavery and later of segregation is that they were genuinely puzzled by the attitudes of their opponents. After all, Southerners didn't approve of the way other Americans ran their affairs, but they didn't try to make those others change. Southerners, it seems to me, are usually willing to let the rest of the country (the world, for that matter) go to hell any way it pleases, and won't interfere unless invited—an attitude learned at home. But it's only reasonable, in this view, to expect that others will keep their missionaries, inspectors, revenue agents, soldiers, and outside agitators at home. If they don't like the way we're living, what's it to them? *Nemo me impune lacessit.*

So what we have, I am suggesting, is a nested set of communities— a region composed of states, composed in turn of cities and towns, themselves made up of groups and associations and neighborhoods, down, in good Burkean fashion, to the level of the family and perhaps beyond. At each level, the criteria for membership and the definitions of the intolerable differ, but everywhere the "love it or leave it" principle applies—even, if we examine the divorce statistics, at the level of the family. The result is communities and groups that enlist the loyalty of their members, so long as they remain members, precisely *because* they are free to leave. W. J. Cash's "savage ideal" of conformity may well characterize relations *within* many Southern communities, while *between* communities a certain rough-and-ready tolerance (indifference, really) prevails.

Of course, this mode of association is, by its nature, centrifugal. The history of the Confederacy, like its existence in the first place, attests to this. The internal tensions, the struggles among the composite states, would have torn the young nation apart, had it not been held together by the common adversary. Just so, the churches of the South have exaggerated the natural tendency of Protestantism to go to seed, dividing over and over again. Groups break away from larger groups, rather than compromise or accommodate. Individuals take their leave as well. But things somehow don't fall apart all that often, or all that disastrously. What holds them together? What countervailing forces check this inherent tendency to disintegration?

In the first place, there is some measure of self-selection. Although nonconformists don't usually have to leave, many choose to. The South has always exported a large proportion of its population to other regions, and it still does. Those who remain, it has been shown, are culturally more "Southern" than those who leave. Although Southern fiction is filled with cranks, grotesques, and weirdos, the South itself doesn't seem to have a great many more than its share. No doubt many have joined the outward migration, and they are now California's problem, or New York's. Similarly, there has always been a great deal of migration *within* the region, originally to the Southwest, more recently from the countryside to the South's cities. It is my impression that misfits and dissenters from the South's smaller communities now tend to migrate to Southern cities, along with the many who go for other reasons, thus preserving the homogeneity and cohesion of the groups they have left behind.

What this means for Southern cities is a different matter. It may mean that big Southern cities will become downright *strange*—nothing new for New Orleans, but surprising to observe in Atlanta and Houston, Nashville and Memphis. The fact that oddballs from the small-town South can often link up with communities of like-minded deviants, and the fact that different communities within Southern cities pretty well succeed in ignoring one another, may mean that most residents of these cities can overlook this development. (It is, in any case, an urban phenomenon and not specifically a Southern one.)

The fact remains that the Southern city is not simply one large community; I am suggesting, furthermore, that the Southern small town was not simply one community either. The two racial groupings are only the most obvious of the many subcommunities within most Southern towns, subcommunities with the ability to mind their own business and to cooperate when circumstances require. The monolithic small-town community may be a New England or a Midwestern phenomenon, but the Southern reality has usually been more complicated than that.

Also operating to offset the tendency toward fragmentation is the frequent presence, sometimes contrived, of external "threat." The South is never more united than when it feels the North is picking on it or pushing it around. I will leave the anthropologists to analyze the solidarity-producing functions of competitive sports but will note, simply for example, that the heterogeneous state of North Carolina is seldom unified except when one of its universities' basketball teams faces outside opposition. At a lower level, the disparate and often hostile subcommunities in small towns unite to support their high school teams against those of other towns. At a higher level, we see the Atlantic Coast Conference *contra mundum.* The structure of Southern athletics, like that of Southern religion, both mirrors and reinforces more general patterns of social organization.

The importance of outsiders in holding things together is reflected in the narrative of the young Tennesseean. His background was far from typically Southern, even in a statistical sense. He came from a part of the South whose Civil War loyalties had been, at best, equivocal, an area with fewer blacks, proportionately, than Boston. His hometown was a busy, dirty industrial city with few reminders of any history before the 1920s, populated mostly by first- and second-generation migrants from other parts of the South. He was raised as a Republican and an Episcopalian (the former minority more acceptable than the latter in his neck of the woods—an inversion of the usual Southern pattern). Yet all these atypical attributes, however important and telling for Southerners, were of no consequence to most Northerners, for whom the overriding datum was simply "Southerner." It could be said that his sense of himself as a member of the regional group was very largely the result of his experiences outside that group. Indeed, his friends who stayed in the South for their educations were generally a good deal less self-conscious about their region than he; many—particularly those who went to the "better" Southern schools—were inclined, in an unreflective way, to be vaguely ashamed of their origins and apologetic about them, anxious to avoid the stigma of provincialism. Paradoxically, it seemed that for this young man and others he knew, travel and residence outside the South led not to assimilation but to a heightened sense of distinctiveness and solidarity with other

Southerners (and the best antidote for a sense of regional inferiority seemed to be exposure to Yankees).

Finally, the South and its constituent groups and communities show more cohesion than we might expect, because they aren't really organized all that consistently with the social ideology I have been describing. The old prescriptive ties, obligations, and hierarchies are disappearing where they have not already vanished, and with them is fading the ideology that justified them and served to offset the implications of the principles of individualism and voluntarism. But the old patterns have been replaced by hierarchies and restraints of a different order, no less real for going unrecognized and unlegitimated by custom and traditional principle. Southern churches, like all formal organizations, exhibit hierarchy and differentiation of function. Southern communities, like all communities, reflect social stratification. And the South's economy is, perhaps more than ever, a complicated, interdependent system in which some command, others obey, and most do both. Whether acknowledged explicitly or not, power remains power, and within the broad limits established by the "love it or leave it" principle, it can still be used to keep others in line.

It is interesting to see how Southerners deal with the facts of stratification, facts that some would say contradict an image of society as made up of autonomous individuals freely acting and in some senses equal. Of course, someone's position in the various hierarchies of Southern society can be attributed partly to his own efforts and decisions. Success, like salvation, has its rewards. On the other hand, Southerners are at least as aware as other Americans that many things are outside their control, that much of what happens to people results from external forces or chance. Since fatalism is one aspect of the now-evaporating traditional value orientation, it may be that Southerners will become more consistent in this respect. Still, it seems to me that we shrink from inflicting on those at the bottom all the scorn, or according to those at the top all the deference, that should follow from a conviction that they deserve to be there. We do not follow through; the harsher implications of our individualism are mitigated by a set of manners that leave a great deal implicit, that even tend to deny the existence of a top and a bottom.

Authority in the South is often veiled by a style that pays lip service to the useful fiction that all men are created equal, whatever the private opinions of those who exercise the authority. W. J. Cash wrote of the old-time Southern industrialist whose back-slapping manner as he mingled with his employees, speaking of hunting and fishing and college football, denied that there was any sharp distinction, much less a qualitative difference, between capitalist and worker. Southern workers have often returned the compliment by refusing to listen to outsiders who insist that there *is* a difference. Similarly, a friend who left the Southern Baptists for the Episcopal church allowed that he preferred a denomination whose bishops were visible (a most unSouthern taste). The Baptists can camouflage their elite; while Anglican bishops may shun the trappings of prelacy, they can hardly escape the designation.

This style is also evident in politics. When President Carter walked in his inaugural parade, when he was sworn in wearing a business suit and came on television in a cardigan sweater, he was solidly in the Southern tradition. (Jefferson's inauguration was also informal, and he was condemned for lacking dignity.) Southerners know who the president is, but we appreciate his not rubbing it in.

Consider as well the folkways of tipping. Expatriate Southerners who have had a New York mailman return all their mail marked AD-DRESSEE UNKNOWN when they didn't know to render a Christmas tribute will recognize that there are regional differences in this matter. Any Northern headwaiter or parking lot attendant will attest that unassimilated Southerners are notoriously poor tippers, and some Southerners more concerned with service than with honor have been known to have friends with less obtrusive accents call for restaurant reservations, or to tip various flunkies in advance.

The point is not that Yankees are greedy or Southerners tight. The difference in customs reflects, rather, a Southern conviction that expecting and receiving tips is demeaning, and somehow unmanly; that giving them can be insulting. When I got my first Southern haircut in some years, I asked cautiously whether North Carolinians tipped barbers yet. "Some do," I was told. "Had a doctor, used to come in here a lot. Always gave me fifty cents." The barber clipped thoughtfully for a while. "Went for a physical one time. Gave *him* fifty cents. 'This is for you, Doc.'" He chuckled. "Seems to me if I want more money I can raise my price." Like the doctor, this man had his skills, his independence, and his pride. He didn't need or intend to depend on the charity of his customers.

Times and mores are changing, perhaps, but the underlying attitude persists. Presents are all right; a present is from one friend, one equal, to another. But tips are for servants, and who would want to be a servant? If you want more money, raise your price. If you don't like it, leave.

Finally, it may even be that the same tendency to deny hierarchy—hierarchy, to repeat, that may very well exist—is evident in Southerners' conversation-starting style. It seems to me that the ice-breaking "What do you do?" is heard less often below the Mason-Dixon Line. Southerners, I think, prefer "Where are you from?" ("What's your sign?"—the West Coast standard—hasn't caught on, even among the singles-bar set.) If Southerners do avoid "What do you do?" this may simply reflect the survival of an older belief that what you *do* is a paltry way to indicate who you *are*. But it's also a matter of manners. To ask that question is to ask someone to brag if he's successful, or to confess failure if he's not. One can like "Where are you from?" for the same reason Melbourne liked the Order of the Garter: because there's no damned merit about it.

In any case, everyone knows there are hierarchies everywhere, in Church, State, and economy. But that fact is unpleasant enough for those at the bottom without their being reminded of it all the time. Those at the top may (in fact, certainly do) feel superior to those at the bottom—why else would they be at the top? But they're obliged not to assault the self-respect of their inferiors by ostentatiously putting them down. Similarly, members of a group may agree among themselves about their group's social or moral superiority to other groups, but they tend to follow forms that keep those opinions tacit, forms that, like the entente among Southern churches, disguise indifference as cordial respect. If, as I believe, race relations are now better in many respects in the South than anywhere else in the country, it may be simply because whites are now prepared to follow these forms in their relations with blacks, as they have always followed them in relations with other whites. And blacks are willing to return the favor.

A final story. A black North Carolinian, now living in New York, once tried to explain why he saw more antiwhite sentiment among

New York blacks than among black Southerners. "Lots of people came here because they wanted to be treated like white folks," he told me. "What they still don't realize is that New Yorkers treat everyone like niggers." Most Southerners are raised to want others to feel at ease, at home, part of the community. Even if we believe their part is an inferior one, even if they are newcomers still on probation, even if they are transients never to be seen again, well-mannered Southerners will try to include them, unless we have reason to believe that they are unassimilable. (Then, of course, we can be as savagely rude as anyone else.) Californians might say we are not sincere; New Yorkers and others who are friendly only to their friends sometimes accuse us of hypocrisy. But it seems to me that we are just trying to deal with the peculiarly modern problem of how to reconcile liberty, equality, and fraternity—a fine but obviously unstable combination. If Southern principles increasingly exalt the first of these, our manners emphasize the second, and the result is a workable version of the third.

What I have been describing is not an abstract blueprint but a way of life, a set of unexamined axioms about the nature of association that I believe are widespread in the South and are likely to remain so. People are free to choose in many important matters, and should bear the consequences. Association is based on shared values and beliefs. People are free to leave associations they find onerous, and should do so. It is impolite to emphasize unavoidable differences in rank. Groups, like individuals, should be free to choose in many matters. Consequently, pluralism and decentralization are desirable policies (a Southern refraction of the Catholic principle of subsidiarity). It is impossible to make a systematic list of these convictions, since they are not so much articulated as lived. Like any way of life, this one embodies contradictions, evasions, and blind spots that rigorous ideologues of any persuasion will likely find intolerable. Never mind. It seems to work, and many of us like it.

More than that, it seems to me that these are among the more important shared understandings that set the young Tennesseean and his fellow Southerners apart from their Northern friends. Not that I claim that this mode of association has always been distinctively Southern; I don't know in what respects it has been that. Many features of it strike me as things the South resisted longer than the rest of the country, that the South adopted only after they had been pretty well abandoned elsewhere. But that doesn't matter. The point is that these are now Southern understandings, in the American context; they are, for the time being, at least, principles that many Southerners find almost instinctively congenial. No doubt many other Americans find those same understandings quaint—or more likely repugnant, since (I have noticed) people who can be perfectly dispassionate when discussing infanticide among the Toda cannot bring a similar detachment to their view of Southern folkways.

I don't insist either that these understandings are somehow at the heart of Southern identity, or that all else depends on them. I doubt that that is true. Details and emphases have changed and will continue to change. Southerners who don't share this view of things, though, may well be uncomfortable in the South (increasingly so, if I am right) and might be happier elsewhere. Recall the bumper-sticker advice to those whose hearts aren't in Dixie.

Clearly, one thing this set of understandings does is to provide a solid rationale—perhaps *underpinning* is the better word—for Southerners' continued insistence on our right as a regional and quasi-ethnic group to keep on doing some things our way, to hold out as a large and gristly lump in the national stew. One thing that sets Southerners off from many other Americans may be the conviction that groups like ours are *entitled* to be set off from the rest.

But however much Southerners may find Southern identity and Southern culture congenial and downright useful, the question remains whether the South has anything to offer the rest of the country. It is an article of the liberal pluralist faith that every group, no matter how apparently degraded, has something to offer the rest of us, that we can all learn from each other. Doesn't this axiom apply to Southerners? To be sure, many who assert this principle most vigorously can, in the next breath, deplore the "Southernization" of America, by which they mean the proliferation of everything from Kentucky Fried Chicken stands and country music to fundamentalist religion and high homicide rates. But they may be right in their assertion, if inconsistent in its application. The South may indeed have something to offer the rest of the country—something other than a bad example, that is.

Alas, as I have explained, it is presumptuous to tell other people how to order their own affairs. Some have abandoned or never subscribed to the principle of individual responsibility, have no respect for self-respect, and regard the world view I have described as hopelessly retrograde. They may have taken a wrong turn, but that is their prerogative. If they have, the consequences will be on them and on their children. So long as we are not obligated to save them from those consequences, they're entitled to the same toleration we have always asked for ourselves. For our part, we should refrain from preaching at them and should seek to construct a society pleasing to man and to God. If we succeed, others can draw the lessons for themselves.

Afterword

For better or for worse, the South has always been an *interesting* place. We needn't fear that it will cease to be interesting just because some of its most conspicuous problems have been solved (or at least palliated to the point where they no longer stick out like a sore thumb). Certainly the social and economic change that has alleviated those problems has come at a bewildering rate in the last few decades, and it has unleashed great forces within the region that will take decades more to work themselves out. Most of this change has been for the better, so far, but there is no denying that most of it has tended to make the South look more like the rest of the United States. In many important ways, consequently, Southerners now look more like other Americans. Their incomes, their housing, their clothing, their racial attitudes—all are less distinctive than they used to be. But in other ways, I wonder.

We often see, elsewhere in the world, that economic development simply provides new ways to do old things, or ways to do what would have been old things if they hadn't been impossible. Japanese use modern birth control to avoid births in unlucky years; Orthodox Jews ride automated elevators on Shabbat; Muslims are summoned to prayer from unbelievable distances by electronic *muezzins*. Not every writer on the South can resist the temptation to treat the region like an American sideshow, and sometimes neither can I, but the following observations are offered more or less seriously, to suggest that the South is surviving what C. Vann Woodward has called "the Bulldozer Revolution" without becoming boring and, indeed, in some cases, that the recent changes have allowed it to manifest its essence in startling new ways:

> An article on snake-handling cults among Appalachian migrants to the lower Midwest reports that the believers have

supplemented their pokey old rattlers and copperheads with genuine imported cobras.

Southern Living magazine advertises "Old South columns" for the homebuilder. They are made of extruded aluminum.

A teenage girl, black, is wearing a sweatshirt emblazoned with the Confederate flag and the legend PROUD TO BE A REBEL. In conversation, she reveals that her Tennessee high school football team are the Rebels, and she is a cheerleader.

The Southern Mansion Massage Parlor in Durham, North Carolina, advertises its "Gone with the Wind atmosphere" in the yellow pages.

Bob Jones University offers its ministerial students a course in "missionary aviation."

The manager of Stuckey's in Coosawatchie, South Carolina, says that "anything with a rebel flag on it is the hottest thing going." The battle flag, at $9.95, is sold almost entirely to Northern tourists. It is made in New Jersey.

Outside the Pass-It-On Christian Book Store and Bait Shop in rural Arkansas is parked a late-model Toyota with a bumper sticker that says SOUTHERNERS DO IT SLOWER.

A television commercial for instant grits addresses the working wife whose husband still demands a hearty breakfast; the Pikeville, Kentucky, Burger Queen attracts a large Sunday after-church crowd with its salad bar, which includes hominy and fried okra; and a newspaper recipe column reports that beaten biscuits are coming back, now that they can be made with a food processor instead of a wooden mallet.

One country singer writes a successful gospel tune with the refrain, "Me and Jesus got our own thing goin'." Another has some success with a song called "Happy Hour Always Makes Me Sad."

A Georgia radio station carries a live remote broadcast from the Midnight Madness Sale at the Dixie Furniture Company. The announcer is named John Wesley Cohen.

"U.S. Out of El Salvador," scrawled on a wall at the University of North Carolina, has been altered to read, "U.S. Out of North Carolina."

No, the South remains, in Cash's words, "not quite a nation within a nation, but the next thing to it." And, as George Orwell pointed out once, national cultures are resilient things, more resilient than even their defenders are likely to allow, "an everlasting animal stretching into the future and the past, and, like all living things, having the power to change out of recognition and yet remain the same." The South has remained the South without slavery, without political independence, without one-party politics, without *de jure* segregation, without an agrarian economy—without all manner of characteristics that were said to be essential. What next?

In fact, change itself may be a continuity of sorts. If Southerners are unusually fond of stability, perhaps it is because they have seen so little of it. Certainly the South has changed faster than the rest of the country in these last few decades, and Southerners are distinguished now (whether or not they were before) by a more extensive experience with rapid social and economic change. This change has disoriented more Southerners than just the old cracker who complained that he never thought he'd see the day he would stand on Peachtree Street and watch colored folks ice-skate. If "future shock" and whatever its consequences may be are not more widespread in the South than elsewhere—if they are not "Southern traits"—they should be.

So the South is not over—not by a long shot. Southern studies will not soon become merely a minor and inconspicuous branch of American studies. Or so it seems to me. To others, of course, all this may sound like whistling in the dark, the brave talk of a professional Dixiologist facing technological unemployment. A lame conclusion, but the only honest one, is that the one thing certain is that we shall see.

Bibliography

Anderson, Don. "At Daniel's Mountain." In Fifteen Southerners, *Why the South Will Survive*. Athens: University of Georgia Press, 1981.

Angoff, Charles, and H. L. Mencken. "The Worst American State." *American Mercury*, XXIV (September, October, November, 1931), 1–16, 177–88, 355–71.

Bertrand, Alvin. "Regional Sociology as a Special Discipline." *Social Forces*, XXXI (1952), 132–36.

Billings, Dwight B. *Planters and the Making of a "New South": Class, Politics, and Development in North Carolina, 1865–1900*. Chapel Hill: University of North Carolina Press, 1979.

Black, Merle. "Is North Carolina Really the 'Best' American State?" In Thad L. Beyle and Merle Black, eds., *Politics and Policy in North Carolina*. New York: MSS Publications, 1975.

Brearley, H. C. "The Pattern of Violence." In W. T. Couch, ed., *Culture in the South*. Chapel Hill: University of North Carolina Press, 1934.

Brooks, Lee M., and Alvin Bertrand. *History of the Southern Sociological Society*. University, Ala.: University of Alabama Press, 1962.

Broom, Leonard, and Norval D. Glenn. "Negro-White Differences in Reported Attitudes and Behavior." *Sociology and Social Research*, I (1966), 187–200.

Campbell, Angus, *et al. The American Voter: An Abridgement*. New York: John Wiley and Sons, 1964.

Carter, Hodding. *Southern Legacy*. Baton Rouge: Louisiana State University Press, 1950.

Cartter, Allan M. *An Assessment of Quality in Graduate Education*. Washington, D.C.: American Council on Education, 1966.

Cash, W. J. *The Mind of the South*. New York: Alfred A. Knopf, 1941.

Davidson, Chandler. *Biracial Politics: Conflict and Coalition in the Metropolitan South*. Baton Rouge: Louisiana State University Press, 1972.

Demerath, Nicholas J. *Social Class in American Protestantism*. Chicago: Rand-McNally, 1965.

Dinnerstein, Leonard, and Mary Dale Palsson, eds. *Jews in the South*. Baton Rouge: Louisiana State University Press, 1973.

Dutton, Jeffrey E., Alan Bayer, and Charles Grigg. "Regional Variation in Academe: The Case of Sociology Faculty in Southern Universities." *Southern Sociologist*, VII (1975), 5–14.

Elkins, Stanley. *Slavery: A Problem in American Institutional and Intellectual Life*. Chicago: University of Chicago Press, 1959.

Environmental Protection Agency. *The Quality of Life Concept: Potential Tool for Decision-Makers*. Washington, D.C.: Environmental Protection Agency, Office of Research and Monitoring [March, 1973].

Fichter, Joseph H., and George Maddox. "Religion in the South, Old and New." In John C. McKinney and Edgar T. Thompson, eds., *The South in Continuity and Change*. Durham, N.C.: Duke University Press, 1965.

Ford, W. Scott. *Interracial Public Housing in Border City: A Situational Analysis of the Contact Hypothesis*. Lexington, Mass.: D. C. Heath Lexington Books, 1972.

Franklin, John Hope. *The Militant South, 1800–1861*. Cambridge: Harvard University Press, 1956.

Garreau, Joel. *The Nine Nations of North America*. Boston: Houghton Mifflin, 1981.

Gastil, Raymond D. *Cultural Regions of the United States*. Seattle: University of Washington Press, 1976.

———. "Homicide and a Regional Culture of Violence." *American Sociological Review*, XXXVI (1971), 412–27.

Glenn, Norval D. "Class and Party Support in the United States: Recent and Emerging Trends." *Public Opinion Quarterly*, XXXVII (1973), 1–20.

———. "Massification Versus Differentiation: Some Trend Data from National Surveys." *Social Forces*, XLVI (1967), 172–80.

———. "Recent Trends in Intercategory Differences in Attitudes." *Social Forces*, LII (1974), 395–401.

———, and J. L. Simmons. "Are Regional Cultural Differences Diminishing?" *Public Opinion Quarterly*, XXXI (1967), 176–93.

Gordon, Milton M. *Assimilation in American Life*. New York: Oxford University Press, 1964.

Gould, Peter R., and Rodney White. *Mental Maps*. Harmondsworth, U.K.: Penguin Books, 1974.

Grasmick, Harold G. "Social Change and the Wallace Movement in the South." Ph.D. Dissertation, University of North Carolina, Chapel Hill, 1973.

Greeley, Andrew M. *Ethnicity in the United States: A Preliminary Reconnaissance*. New York: John Wiley and Sons, 1974.

Hackney, Sheldon. "Southern Violence." *American Historical Review*, LXXIV (1969), 906–25.

Harding, John et al. "Prejudice and Ethnic Relations." In Gardner Lindzey and Elliot Aronson, eds., *Handbook of Social Psychology*. Vol. V. 2nd ed. Reading, Mass.: Addison-Wesley, 1969.

Heberle, Rudolf. "Regionalism: Some Critical Observations." *Social Forces*, XXI (1943), 280–86.

Hemphill, Paul. *The Good Old Boys*. New York: Simon & Schuster, 1974.

Hero, Alfred O. *The Southerner and World Affairs*. Baton Rouge: Louisiana State University Press, 1965.

Hertzler, J. O. "Some Notes on the Social Psychology of Regionalism." *Social Forces*, XVIII (1940), 331–37.

Hill, Samuel S., Jr. *Southern Churches in Crisis*. New York: Holt, Rinehart and Winston, 1967.

Hobbs, S. H., Jr. *North Carolina: Economic and Social*. Chapel Hill: University of North Carolina Press, 1930.

Hunter, Floyd. *Community Power Structure*. Chapel Hill: University of North Carolina Press, 1953.

Isaacs, Harold R. *Idols of the Tribe: Group Identity and Political Change*. New York: Harper and Row, 1975.

Janowitz, Morris. *The Professional Soldier: A Social and Political Portrait*. New York: Free Press, 1960.

Jensen, Merrill, ed. *Regionalism in America*. 2nd ed. Madison: University of Wisconsin Press, 1965.

Katz, Daniel, and Kenneth Braley. "Racial Stereotypes of One Hundred College Students." *Journal of Abnormal and Social Psychology*, XXVIII (1933), 280–90.

Kelly, Clarence M. *Crime in the United States: 1972*. Washington, D.C.: Government Printing Office, 1973.

Key, V. O., Jr. *Southern Politics in State and Nation*. New York: Alfred A. Knopf, 1949.

Killian, Lewis. *White Southerners*. New York: Random House, 1970.

Kirby, Jack Temple. *Media-Made Dixie: The South in the American Imagination*. Baton Rouge: Louisiana State University Press, 1978.

Kollmorgen, Walter. "Crucial Deficiencies of Regionalism." *American Economic Review*, XXXV (1945), 377–89.

Lenski, Gerhard. *The Religious Factor*. Garden City, N.Y.: Doubleday, 1961.

LePlay, Frédéric. *Les ouvriers européens*. 2nd ed. Tours: A. Mame et fils, 1877–79.

Lippmann, Walter. *Public Opinion*. New York: Harcourt, Brace, 1922.

Lipset, Seymour Martin, and Everett C. Ladd, Jr. "Jewish Academics in the United States: Their Achievements, Culture, and Politics." In American Jewish Committee, *American Jewish Yearbook, 1971*. Vol. LXXII. Philadelphia: Jewish Publication Society of America, 1971.

Liu, Ben-Chieh. *The Quality of Life in the United States*. Kansas City: Midwest Research Institute, 1973.

Loftin, Colin, and Robert H. Hill. "Regional Subculture and Homicide: An Examination of the Gastil-Hackney Thesis." *American Sociological Review*, XXXIX (1974), 714–24.

Maclachlan, John. "Distinctive Cultures in the Southeast: Their Possibilities for Regional Research." *Social Forces*, XVIII (1939), 210–15.

Matthews, Donald, and James Prothro. *Negroes and the New Southern Politics*. New York: Harcourt, Brace & World, 1966.

McDavid, Raven I. *Varieties of American English*. Stanford, Calif.: Stanford University Press, 1980.

McKinney, John C., and Linda B. Bourque. "The Changing South: National Incorporation of a Region." *American Sociological Review*, XXXVI (1971), 399–412.

"Measuring the Quality of Life in America: A New Frontier for Social Science." *Newsletter* [Institute for Social Research, University of Michigan], II (Summer, 1974), 3–8.

Merton, Robert K., Patricia S. West, and Marie Jahoda. "Social Fictions and Social Facts: The Dynamics of Race Relations in Hilltown." Mimeographed report. Columbia University Bureau of Applied Social Research, New York, 1949.

Mitchell, Broadus, and George Sinclair Mitchell. *The Industrial Revolution in the South*. Baltimore: Johns Hopkins Press, 1930.

Morland, J. Kenneth, ed. *The Not So Solid South: Anthropological Studies in a Regional Subculture*. Athens: University of Georgia Press, 1971.

Morris, Willie, ed. *The South Today: 100 Years After Appomattox*. New York: Harper and Row, 1965.

Murray, Albert. *South to a Very Old Place*. New York: McGraw-Hill, 1971.

Myrdal, Gunnar. *An American Dilemma*. Twentieth Anniversary Edition. New York: Harper, 1962.

Nisbet, Robert. *The Sociological Tradition*. New York: Basic Books, 1966.

O'Brien, Michael. *The Idea of the American South, 1920–1941*. Baltimore: Johns Hopkins Press, 1979.

O'Connor, Flannery. *Mystery and Manners: Occasional Prose*. Edited by Sally Fitzgerald and Robert Fitzgerald. New York: Farrar, Straus & Giroux, 1969.

Odum, Howard W. *An American Epoch: Southern Portraiture in the National Picture*. New York: Henry Holt, 1930.

––––––. *Folk, Region, and Society: Selected Papers of Howard W. Odum*. Edited by Katherine Jocher et al. Chapel Hill: University of North Carolina Press, 1964.

––––––. *Southern Regions of the United States*. Chapel Hill: University of North Carolina Press, 1936.

––––––. *The Way of the South*. New York: Macmillan, 1947.

––––––, and Harry Estill Moore. *American Regionalism: A Cultural-Historical Approach to National Integration*. New York: Henry Holt, 1938.

––––––, and Katherine Jocher, eds. *In Search of the Regional Balance of America*. Chapel Hill: University of North Carolina Press, 1945.

Olsen, Stephen M. "Regional Social Systems: Linking Quantitative Analysis with Field Work." In *Regional Analysis*. Vol. II: *Social Systems*. New York: Academic Press, 1976.

Orwell, George. *The Lion and the Unicorn: Socialism and the English Genius*. London: Secker & Warburg, 1941.

Parsons, Talcott. *The Social System*. New York: Free Press, 1964 [1951].

Peterson, Richard A., and Paul DiMaggio. "From Region to Class, the Changing Locus of Country Music: A Test of the Massification Hypothesis." *Social Forces*, LIII (1975), 497–506.

Phillips, Ulrich B. *American Negro Slavery: A Survey of the Supply, Employment, and Control of Negro Labor as Determined by the Plantation Regime*. Baton Rouge: Louisiana State University Press, 1966 [1918].

———. "The Central Theme of Southern History." *American Historical Review*, XXXIV (1928), 30–43.

Podhoretz, Norman. "How the North Was Won." *New York Times Magazine*, September 30, 1979, pp. 20, 50–64.

Potter, David. *The South and the Sectional Conflict*. Baton Rouge: Louisiana State University Press, 1968.

Powledge, Fred. *Journeys Through the South: A Rediscovery*. New York: Vanguard Press, 1979.

Raper, Arthur. *The Tragedy of Lynching*. Chapel Hill: University of North Carolina Press, 1933.

Reddick, L. D. "The Negro as Southerner and American." In Charles Grier Sellers, Jr., ed., *The Southerner as American*. New York: E. P. Dutton, 1966.

Reed, John Shelton. *The Enduring South: Subcultural Persistence in Mass Society*. Lexington, Mass.: D. C. Heath Lexington Books, 1971.

———. "Needles in Haystacks: Studying 'Rare' Populations by Secondary Analysis of National Sample Surveys." *Public Opinion Quarterly*, XXXIX (1975–76), 514–22.

Riemer, Svend. "Theoretical Aspects of Regionalism." *Social Forces*, XXI (1943), 275–80.

Sharkansky, Ira. *Regionalism in American Politics*. Indianapolis: Bobbs-Merrill, 1970.

Shils, Edward. "Primordial, Personal, Sacred, and Civil Ties." *British Journal of Sociology*, VIII (1957), 130–45.

Singal, Daniel. *The War Within: From Victorian to Modernist Thought in the South, 1919–1945*. Chapel Hill: University of North Carolina Press, 1982.

Thernstrom, Stephan, ed. *Harvard Encyclopedia of American Ethnic Groups*. Cambridge: Harvard University Press, 1980.

Thompson, Edgar T. *Plantation Societies, Race Relations, and the South: The Regimentation of Populations*. Durham, N.C.: Duke University Press, 1975.

Tindall, George Brown. *The Ethnic Southerners*. Baton Rouge: Louisiana State University Press, 1976.

Triandis, Harry C. *Attitude and Attitude Change*. New York: John Wiley and Sons, 1971.

———. "Frequency of Contact and Stereotyping." *Journal of Personality and Social Psychology*, VII (1967), 316–28.

Twelve Southerners. *I'll Take My Stand: The South and the Agrarian Tradition*. Baton Rouge: Louisiana State University Press, 1977 [1930].

Vance, Rupert B. "The Geography of Distinction: The Nation and Its Regions, 1790–1927." *Social Forces*, XVIII (1939), 168–79.

———. *Human Geography of the South*. Chapel Hill: University of North Carolina Press, 1932.

———. *Regionalism and the South: Selected Papers of Rupert Vance*. Edited by John Shelton Reed and Daniel Singal. Chapel Hill: University of North Carolina Press, 1982.

———. "Sociological Implications of Southern Regionalism." *Journal of Southern History*, XXVI (1960), 44–56.

———, and Waller Wynne, Jr. "Folk Rationalizations in the 'Unwritten Law.'" *American Journal of Sociology*, XXXIX (1933), 483–92.

Walls, David. "Central Appalachia: A Peripheral Region Within an Advanced Capitalist Society." *Journal of Sociology and Social Welfare*, IV (1976), 232–47.

Westie, Frank R. "Academic Expectations for Professional Immortality: A Study of Legitimation." *American Sociologist*, VIII (1973), 19–32.

Whitfield, Stephen J. "Jews and Other Southerners: Counterpoint and Paradox." In Nathan M. Kaganoff and Melvin I. Urofsky, eds., *"Turn to the South": Essays on Southern Jewry*. Charlottesville: University Press of Virginia, 1979.

Williams, Robin M., Jr. *Strangers Next Door: Ethnic Relations in American Communities*. Englewood Cliffs, N.J.: Prentice-Hall, 1964.

Wolfgang, Marvin E., and Franco Ferracuti. "Subculture of Violence: An Integrated Conceptualization." In David O. Arnold, ed., *The Sociology of Subcultures*. Berkeley: Glendessary Press, 1970.

Woodward, C. Vann. *The Burden of Southern History*. Baton Rouge: Louisiana State University Press, 1968.

Zelinsky, Wilbur. *The Cultural Geography of the United States*. Englewood Cliffs, N.J.: Prentice-Hall, 1973.

———. "Cultural Variations in Personal Name Patterns in the Eastern United States." *Annals of the Association of American Geographers*, LX (1970), 743–49.

———. "North America's Vernacular Regions." *Annals of the Association of American Geographers*, LXX (1980), 1–16.

———. "Selfward Bound? Personal Preference Patterns and the Changing Map of American Society." *Economic Geography*, L (1974), 144–79.

Index

Agrarians, 7, 154–55, 162–63, 168, 169, 174

Agriculture: as determinant of Southern culture, 24, 25, 37, 73, 130, 166, 170–71, 188; and modernization of South, 129, 162, 165, 166, 170–71, 188

Alabama, 20, 71, 154, 156, 158

American Sociological Association, 33–34, 46

Anderson, Don, 113

Appalachia: as distinct subregion of South, 14, 20, 42; regional identification in, 17, 20, 21, 82; interest of regional sociologists in, 38, 39; exclusion of, from Dixie, 69, 73, 76; mentioned, 19, 146

Arkansas, 67, 69, 158

Asheville, N.C., 69, 73

Atlanta, Ga.: exclusion of, from Dixie, 68, 69, 73–75; as model of "New South," 73–75, 130, 133; violence in, 139, 139n; mentioned, 165, 178

Babbitt, Irving, 131

Bakersfield, Calif., 148, 148n

Baltimore, Md., 139

Baptist church, 29, 82, 120, 134, 135, 172, 181

Baton Rouge, La., 73, 122, 165

Bertrand, Alvin, 33–34, 37, 42

Billings, Dwight, 40

Birmingham, Ala., 75

Black, Merle, 6–7, 156

Blacks: Southern identification of, 6–7, 18, 21, 113–18, 166; regional variation among, 15, 53, 55; and white Southerners, 18, 31; level of group identification among, 21, 41, 78, 80; effect of, on Southern culture and identification, 24–26, 31,

73, 82; stereotyping of, 88, 89; manifestation of elements of Southern culture among, 134, 153, 157, 171; migration of, into South, 156; mentioned, 14, 42, 169, 182–83. *See also* Race relations; Segregation

Bontemps, Arna, 113

Braley, Kenneth, 88, 95

Brearley, H. C., 146

California, 15, 31, 156, 157

Campbell, Angus, 79

Carter, Billy, 120, 121, 147

Carter, Hodding, 145–46

Carter, Jimmy, 32, 54, 120, 121, 133, 181

Carter, Miz Lillian, 120–21

Cash, Johnny, 149, 151

Cash, W. J., 4, 54, 141, 177, 188

Charleston, S.C., 67, 68

Charlotte, N.C., 132, 133, 140

Chicago, Ill., 65, 140, 148

Civil rights movement, 55, 116, 138. *See also* Race relations; Segregation

Civil War, 166–67

Clower, Jerry, 51

Cole, William, 47

Columbia, S.C., 132–33

Columbia University, 47

Columbus, Ga., 139

Community. *See* Localism, as part of Southern culture

Comparative State Elections Project, 156

Comte, August, 46

Congregationalism, 29, 176

Connecticut, 154, 158

Contact hypothesis. *See* Stereotyping, and contact hypothesis

Coulter, Janice, 45

Country music, 32, 50, 147, 148–50, 184